Drawing Shadows to Stone

The Yukaghir people of northeastern Siberia, seeing a camera for the first time, called it "the three-legged device that draws a person's shadow to stone." The three legs were the tripod, and the shadow drawn to stone was the image inscribed onto the glass-plate negative. The photographer's shadow can be seen at lower right. (1623)

DRAWING SHADOWS TO STONE

The Photography of the Jesup North Pacific Expedition, 1897–1902

Laurel Kendall, Barbara Mathé, Thomas Ross Miller

with Stanley A. Freed, Ruth S. Freed *&* Laila Williamson

American Museum of Natural History   *New York*

in association with the University of Washington Press   *Seattle & London*

Published in conjunction with the exhibition *Drawing Shadows to Stone,*
curated by Barbara Mathé and Thomas Ross Miller and organized by the
American Museum of Natural History.

This publication was made possible in part by a grant from the
Joan Paterson Kerr Fund.

Designed by Audrey Meyer
Printed in Hong Kong

Published simultaneously in Canada by Douglas & McIntyre,
Vancouver/Toronto.

Library of Congress Cataloging-in-Publication Data

Drawing shadows to stone : the photography of the Jesup North Pacific
Expedition 1897–1902 / Laurel Kendall . . . [et al.].
p.   cm.
Includes bibliographical references and index.
ISBN 0-295-97647-0 (alk. paper)
1. Photography in ethnology—Canada—History.   2. Photography
in ethnology—Russia (Federation)—Siberia—History.   3. Jesup North
Pacific Expedition (1897–1903)   4. American Museum of Natural
History—Photograph collections.   I. Kendall, Laurel.   II. Jesup North
Pacific Expedition (1897–1903).   III. American Museum of Natural
History.
GN347.D73   1997   97-13050
305.8—dc21   CIP

The paper used in this publication meets the minimum requirements of
American National Standard for Information Sciences—Permanence of
Paper for Printed Library Materials, ANSI Z39.48-1984. ∞

Contents

A female shaman of the Koryak people. (337173)

Preface: Exotic Images and Early Anthropological Photographs

Up to about the second decade of this century photography was, broadly speaking,
part of the collective endeavor in the production of anthropological data.
—*Elizabeth Edwards*

ETWEEN 1897 and 1902 the men and women of the Jesup North Pacific Expedition produced some three thousand photographs from the peoples of the northwest coast of Canada and the northeastern coast of Siberia. Photography was an integral component of American anthropology's foremost ethnographic expedition. How does one "read" these images today? How were they meant to be read when they were produced one hundred years ago?

What does one see in *any* antique photograph of a distant place? At the end of the twentieth century, we know better than to take late nineteenth- and early twentieth-century photography at face value. Edward S. Curtis unabashedly dressed his Native American subjects with his own costumes and props to create romantic portraits of the "noble savage" (Blackman 1980; Lyman 1982). Photographing exotic images of San Francisco's old Chinatown, Arnold Genthe effaced from his prints English-language shop signs and persons in western dress (Tchen 1984). In Malek Alloula's *The Colonial Harem* (1986), picture postcards of sensuously posed Algerian women document nothing of Algeria so much as the erotic imagination of its French colonizers.

A very thin line divides the production of exotic images for popular consumption from anthropological photography. Some of the photographers who worked with anthropological expeditions also produced commercial images, and many ethnographic photographs have appeared in popular publications such as *National Geographic* (Blackman 1980). As Barbara Mathé and Thomas Ross Miller remind us in their essay "Drawing Shadows to Stone," ethnographers who saw themselves as recording vanishing traditional cultures struggled to excise evidence of contact and assimilation from the frames of their compositions. They posed their subjects at activities that would be replicated in future museum exhibits and recorded them, dressed and undressed, in awkward front and side views, as racial-type data, uncomfortable artifacts of the arrogance of a young science (Miller and Mathé, this volume; Jacknis 1984).

While the Jesup Expedition photographs have clear parallels in the "subjective," "contrived," and even "pornographic" images of early popular photography, such judgments are ultimately facile if we take them as the last word, ignoring the photographers' own intentions. Elizabeth Edwards describes early anthropology as more visually oriented than the professional discipline that developed in the first half of the twentieth century. Early anthropologists set great value upon tangible things as cultural data. Photographs were of a piece with artifacts, anthropometric measurements, head casts, sound recordings, and linguistic transcripts (Edwards 1992; Jacknis 1984:3).

By contrast, the founding fathers of modern professional anthropology—Boas, Malinowski, and Radcliffe-Brown—would conceptualize "culture" as something that exists "in people's heads," as abstract understandings that might be apprehended only through long-term residence with a people and a high degree of linguistic competence. Visual representations of culture, as embodied in museum dioramas, were necessarily partial, insufficient, or superficial (Edwards 1992; Jacknis 1985). While the monographs produced by members of the Jesup Expedition were richly illustrated with images of people and artifacts, it now became possible to publish an ethnography without a single photograph.* "Visual anthropology" evolved as a discrete sub-discipline rather than a part of the common pursuit (Edwards 1992).

The Jesup Expedition bridged this transition. In designing the project, Franz Boas drew upon the methods and technologies of expedition anthropology, but he had begun to conceptualize culture as far more than the sum of its material and measurable components (Boas 1940; Jacknis 1985; Stocking 1974). The Jesup Expedition photographs are most richly read through an understanding of how early anthropologists with cameras saw both their task and their science—as will be illuminated in the text and images that follow. At a moment when anthropologists, encouraged by the accessibility of video and new electronic media, have begun once again to celebrate the visual, we can also "read" these old photographs as a measure of the many transformations that continue to take place within anthropological practice.

* Eleven volumes of the Memoirs of the American Museum of Natural History, Jesup North Pacific Expedition, edited by Franz Boas, were published sequentially between 1898 and 1930 (New York: American Museum of Natural History). The series includes research by Franz Boas, Waldemar Bogoras, Livingston Farrand, Gerard Fowke, George Hunt, Waldemar Jochelson, Berthold Laufer, Harlan Smith, John R. Swanton, James Teit, and Bruno Oetteking. Lev Iakovlevich Shternberg's previously unpublished manuscript, "The Social Organization of the Gilyak," edited by Bruce Grant, will be the final volume in this series.

I wish to thank Stanley Freed for his reading of this essay.

Laurel Kendall

Curator, Asian Ethnographic Collections, American Museum of Natural History

Tough Fieldworkers: History and Personalities of the Jesup Expedition

Stanley A. Freed, Ruth S. Freed, and Laila Williamson

THE JESUP North Pacific Expedition was organized in 1897 to investigate the origin of the American Indians. Teams of scientists operated on both sides of the Bering Strait, the presumed route of migration from Asia to North America. The ambitious, multidisciplinary project immediately captured the popular imagination. In an editorial on March 14, 1897, the *New York Times* acclaimed the question of Amerindian origins as "about the biggest of the unsolved anthropological and ethnical problems" and "alive with human and historic interest."

Although the question of Amerindian origins is interesting, this scientific problem alone does not account for the enduring fascination of the Jesup Expedition. The expedition also had a compelling dramatic quality. Half of it was carried out in Siberia, one of the world's harshest environments. It featured remarkable personalities, men and women who led unusual and adventurous lives. In Russia, the research took place at the beginning of one of the most important revolutionary periods in world history. On the American side, the expedition followed two decades of railroad building, which tied the country together and opened the West. A burgeoning economy and the expansion of the railroad system placed vast wealth in the hands of men who liked big ideas. Such a man was Morris K. Jesup (1830–1908), president of the American Museum of Natural History and sponsor of the expedition that bears his name.

Born in Connecticut, Jesup had a secure, conventional childhood that ended when his family lost its fortune in the panic of 1837 and his father died the same year. His mother moved the family to New York, where she struggled to raise eight children. At the age of twelve, Jesup left school to work as an office boy. When he was twenty-four, he started a small business that handled railroad supplies. Three years later, he founded a new railroad supply firm that gradually drifted into banking, and it was in banking and railroad finance that he made his fortune. At age fifty-four, he retired from banking to devote his wealth and energy to public service. He served as president of the American Museum from 1881 until his death almost twenty-seven years later. He purchased collections, sponsored research, and gave generously to the American Museum.

Franz Boas (1858–1942), a young assistant curator in the Museum's Department of Anthropology, conceived and organized the Jesup Expedition and was its guiding force. Born and educated in Germany, Boas emigrated to the United States as a young man. He was interested both in the tribes of the Siberian coast and those of the north Pacific coast of America from Puget Sound to Alaska, a region known as the Northwest Coast. He began his own research on the Northwest Coast in 1886 with a three-month visit to Vancouver Island, and continued his work with five brief field trips from 1888 to 1895. After he was turned down for a post in the new Columbian Museum of Chicago (now the Field Museum of Natural History), Boas lived by contract work until he was hired by the American Museum in

Morris K. Jesup, trustee, charter member, and third president of the American Museum of Natural History. (2A5200)

1896, at the urging of Frederic W. Putnam, who was then in charge of the Department of Anthropology.

Boas realized that the president of the American Museum and the wealthy members of its board of trustees could be enlisted to support research and collecting. He persuaded Putnam to support a six-year project of research on both sides of the Bering Strait. The two men then presented the idea to Jesup. Knowing that Jesup liked big projects and major scientific problems, Putnam and Boas wisely appealed to this aspect of his personality, arguing that the expedition would settle the question of the origin of the first immigrants to the New World. Jesup liked the idea and agreed to bear all the expenses of the project.

Although Jesup and the popular press were interested chiefly in the origin of the American Indians, Boas seemed little concerned with it, probably because their Asiatic origin seemed obvious. Instead, he planned to focus on the physical and cultural relationships between the peoples of Siberia and the New World. He was looking for universal laws of cultural development. In his earliest statement of the purposes of the expedition, a letter published in *Globus* in 1897, Boas said,

> Besides the general ethnological interest of the study, I find the question of the geographical distribution of ethnological phenomena to be especially important. I believe that our science urgently needs to examine the historical development of primitive culture to arrive at a clear understanding of the rules of cultural development.

On the American side, the research was carried out by professional anthropologists, supplemented by amateurs under Boas's direction. These field investigators collected a formidable amount of data and published most of it. Harlan I. Smith, who served at the American Museum until 1911 and eventually became Chief Archaeologist of the National Museum of Canada, excavated sites in British Columbia and Washington State. John R. Swanton, who studied the Haida Indians early in his career while a member of the Jesup Expedition, was in the course of time to produce a prodigious body of publications on the North American Indians. Livingston Farrand of Columbia University wrote on the traditions of the Chilcotin and Quinault and on the basketry designs of several Salish groups. The chief investigator on the American side of the Bering Strait was Boas himself. In addition to his famous monographs on the Kwakiutl (now called Kwakwa̱ka̱'wakw), Boas wrote about the Nuxalk (Bella Coola) and edited the Jesup series.

Boas's local collaborators, James Teit and George Hunt, straddled Eurocanadian and Indian cultures. Their contributions were unique and substantial. Teit, a Scotsman from Spences Bridge who married a Thompson Indian woman, spoke several Salish dialects fluently. He wrote on the Thompson (a group now known as Nlaka'pamux), Lillooet, and Shuswap. George Hunt was even more closely

Franz Boas. (2A5161)

George Hunt, 1898. Photo by H. I. Smith. (11854)

identified with the Indian world. His mother was a Tlingit and his father, an English Hudson's Bay Company factor. Raised in Fort Rupert as a Kwakwaka'wakw, Hunt spoke their language fluently, was literate in English, and was a steady and reliable worker. Much of Boas's research depended on him. Boas trained him to transcribe Kwakwaka'wakw texts, and his name appears with Boas's on the title pages of the monographs that deal with these texts.

Intense competition—enhanced by personal bitterness—between New York's American Museum and Chicago's Columbian Museum was a sidelight of the work in British Columbia. Boas felt that his rejection at Chicago was an "unsurpassed insult," and Putnam shared his anger. With Jesup's wealth behind them, Putnam and Boas were in a strong position in New York, and Putnam vowed to "show Chicago I can go them one better" (Dexter 1976:306). George A. Dorsey at the Columbian Museum also had solid financial backing and was as combative as the New Yorkers. He wrote, "At the present time they have at least twenty-seven [totem] poles in New York and we have twenty-three in Chicago. I do not like to have the difference in number remain against us" (Cole 1985:288).

From Boas's point of view, the most threatening aspect of this competition was Dorsey's attempt to raid Boas's team, especially his effort to lure George Hunt. Boas knew it would be very difficult to find a replacement with Hunt's qualifications. In addition to contending with Dorsey, Boas had occasional problems with the Kwakwaka'wakw. The *New York Herald* (Oct. 31, 1897) published a long story based on an interview with Boas about the ritual behavior of the Cannibal Spirit dancer. The sense of the interview was distorted by sensational headlines: "Fierce Kwakiutls Who Practise Cannibalism in North America, As Seen By Dr. Boas." The Kwakwaka'wakw were displeased and for a time barred Hunt from observing their ceremonies. Boas responded in typical Kwakwaka'wakw style by giving a feast and managed to restore cordial relations.

The conditions of research on the Russian side of the Bering Strait were much more difficult than on the

James Teit and his wife, Lucy Antko. Photo c. 1896. (11686)

Three teams carried out the fieldwork: one in the Amur River region and two in northeastern Siberia and Kamchatka. The ethnologist Berthold Laufer (1874–1934) was in charge of the Amur River team, whose other member was Gerard Fowke (1855–1933), an American archaeologist. Born in Germany, Laufer was well qualified for work in Asia, having studied no fewer than ten Asian languages. Laufer happily accepted Boas's offer of $500 per year plus field expenses to study the tribes living along the Amur River and on Sakhalin Island.

Although Boas easily reached an agreement with Laufer, securing Russian permission for his work in Siberia was another matter. Laufer was a Jew, and Jewish birth was anathema to the tsarist government. Jesup had to seek the intervention of the U.S. Department of State to obtain the necessary visa. E. Hitchcock of the American Embassy in St. Petersburg wrote to Jesup confirming that to issue a visa to Laufer would be against the law, "Dr. Laufer being a German Jew." Hitchcock took the matter to several sympathetic Russian scientists: V. Radloff, director of the Museum of Anthropology and Ethnography of the Imperial Academy of Sciences, who called upon the Grand Duke Constantin, President of the Academy, who in turn directed Radloff to the Governor General of Siberia. Shortly thereafter, Hitchcock could report that the visa would be issued "by special permission of his Majesty the Emperor" (AMNH, Hitchcock to Jesup, April 23, 1898).

Laufer had a taste for fieldwork and for the most part stoically endured its hardships. However, there were some frightening illnesses and accidents, among them a two-and-a-half-month siege of influenza and pneumonia and a plunge through weak ice into frigid water that would have been fatal had not his guide been there to save him. Concerning fieldwork on the lower Amur, Laufer wrote, "Nobody who has not been there can have an idea of the dreadful horrors one has to undergo" (DA, Laufer to Boas, November 2, 1899). Explaining to Boas how costly work on the Amur River would be, Laufer observed, "Nothing is free here except death, which you can have in this country at

American side, where the Canadians and Americans had to deal chiefly with some inter-museum competition and a few contentious matters with the Indians. In Siberia, climate, terrain, illness, and vast distances that had to be covered by horse, reindeer sled, dog sled, boat, and raft, or on foot made research a dangerous adventure. It called forth a toughness that is rarely required in the present age of modern transport and communication. Moreover, some Russian governmental policies were an obstacle. The Canadian and American governments took no interest in the activities of Boas's team, but would help if asked. The Russian government took a definite and hostile interest in the three principal investigators in Siberia: Berthold Laufer, Waldemar Bogoras, and Waldemar Jochelson.

special bargain rates" (DA, Laufer to Boas, March 4, 1899; see also Kendall 1988).

Fowke, Laufer's colleague, was largely a self-taught adventurer, drawn to archaeology by his love for outdoor life and taste for exotic customs. With two companions, he set out to explore the Amur River by boat from Verkhne-Tambovsk to Nikolayevsk at the mouth of the river, a distance of about 330 miles. The rigors of the trip were almost too much for the American outdoorsman and adventurer. He complained about impenetrable vegetation and about insects, writing that "flies that bite like mosquitoes. . . . swarmed in millions: mosquitoes were in clouds" (DA, Fowke to Boas, September 15, 1989).

The Amur River team achieved less than might be expected, especially when its output is compared to the classic ethnographies produced by Bogoras and Jochelson of the northern team. Laufer collected many objects that are superb artworks, but his only publication in the Jesup North Pacific Expedition series is a well-illustrated study of decorative motifs, rather than the intended comprehensive ethnography. After the Jesup Expedition, Laufer led the Jacob H. Schiff Expedition to China in 1901–04. He made two other prolonged visits to the Far East for scholarly purposes: in 1908–10 as leader of the Blackstone Expedition to Tibet and China and in 1923 on the Marshall Field Expedition to China. In 1908 Laufer joined Chicago's Field Museum of Natural History, where he spent the remainder of his scholarly career. For many years he was easily the outstanding American sinologist.

Fowke's work, as he himself acknowledged, was a "dismal fizzle." Boas considered him to have been a mistake and permitted him only one season in Siberia. Fowke returned to the United States, where he continued his archaeological research well into his seventies.

On the recommendation of Radloff, Boas entrusted the fieldwork in northern Siberia to Waldemar I. Jochelson (1855–1937) and Waldemar G. Bogoras (1865–1936) who, unlike Laufer and Fowke, were already veterans of several years of Siberian research when they joined the Jesup Expe-

dition. Friends and colleagues, they were Russian intellectuals and revolutionaries who in their youth were exiled to Siberia where they became ethnographers.* They belonged to Narodnaya Volya (Peoples' Will), a radical, populist, and revolutionary political party. They both believed that ethnography represented the intellectual path to populism.

Jochelson left Russia in 1880 but tried to return illegally in 1885. He was recognized at the border, arrested, imprisoned for two years, and then exiled to the Yakut (Sakha) District in Siberia for ten years. While there, he became interested in the customs of the Skoptsy, a fanatic religious sect also exiled to Siberia. Its members believed that only castration could assure them eternal salvation. Jochelson's published notes on the Skoptsy caught the attention of the scientific community. Shortly thereafter, the head of the Eastern Siberian Department of the Russian Geographic Society proposed him for the Sibiriakov Expedition (1895–97) to the Sakha District, organized by and named after its patron, I. M. Sibiriakov (Gurvich and Kuzmina 1985:148).

Bogoras joined Peoples' Will in 1882 at the age of seventeen. He was arrested for revolutionary activity and imprisoned in Taganrog, where he had grown up. After his release, he went underground, changing his given names from Nathan Mendelevich to Waldemar Germanovich and adopting the Orthodox faith. However, his first name became his literary pseudonym, N. A. Tan. He was again arrested, imprisoned for three years, and then exiled for ten years to the town of Sredne-Kolymsk in the Kolyma region, where he arrived in 1889.

* It was nothing new for Russian political exiles in Siberia to become ethnographers. The Decembrists, whose mutiny in December 1825 in St. Petersburg was quickly crushed, represented the Russian elite. Five of them were hung and 111 were exiled to Siberia. The work of those who became ethnographers was considered equal to the other ethnographic work of the time. The Decembrists may be ranked among the founders of Siberian ethnography (Troubetzkoy 1980:136, 169). We thank Professor Piero Matthey, Universita' di Torino, for calling our attention to Troubetzkoy's article and providing other information in his letter of April 18, 1989.

Sredne-Kolymsk's inhabitants were descendants of Cossack explorers, who had settled there in the seventeenth and eighteenth centuries. They had long lived in the middle of a non-Russian native population, adopting native economic activities and other customs useful in the Arctic. But they preserved their own language and customs and never lost their ethnic identity. Bogoras collected and published their folklore. Specialists took an interest in the young researcher, and in 1895 he was, like Jochelson, invited to participate in the Sibiriakov Expedition (Gurvich and Kuzmina 1985:145).

Bogoras was proud that he, Jochelson, and Leo Shternberg, a third exile, had not perished either physically or mentally during ten very difficult years in Siberia. The three men were in St. Petersburg in 1898–99 when Boas was searching for people to carry out the Siberian phase of the Jesup Expedition. Bogoras and Jochelson were appointed immediately on Radloff's recommendation, and Shternberg joined the expedition several years later, to study the Gilyak (see Vakhtin 1994).

The Russian government considered Bogoras's and Jochelson's revolutionary background to be a serious problem and reacted by issuing contradictory orders. Two documents were similar open letters, one to Bogoras and one to Jochelson, from Tsar Nicholas II, charging those in the Ministry of the Interior "to render . . . all possible aid within their lawful powers" to enable the men to discharge their mission. The other document was a confidential circular:

To the Chiefs of the District Police of the Yakutsk Province. In compliance with a confidential letter of the Minister of the Interior . . . the Military Governor-General of the Province of Irkutsk . . . has requested me to take measures to establish a secret surveillance over the acts of Wladimir Bogoras and Wladimir Jochelson, former administrative exiles. . . . it [is] entirely unwarranted to render them assistance of any kind in the scientific work assigned to them.

Jochelson and Bogoras came to New York in March 1900 to prepare for their May departure for Siberia. On

March 24, Jesup wrote a long letter to Jochelson officially giving him charge of the work of the expedition in northeastern Siberia, describing its purposes and detailing its finances. Each man would receive $100 per month and expenses. Their wives would accompany them and contribute to the scientific work of the expedition. The women would receive no pay, but Jesup agreed to advance money for their expenses, such funds to be deducted from the salaries paid to their husbands at the final accounting.

Arriving at Mariinsky Post at the mouth of the Anadyr River in July 1900, the Bogorases spent their first four months of fieldwork with the Reindeer Chukchi, who camped along the seashore during the summer. Bogoras casually described conditions that summer as rather "unfavorable" because of a measles epidemic which, in places, killed 30 percent of the population. At the end of October he began a journey with a Cossack and a native guide through a territory ranging from Indian Point and St. Lawrence Island on the northeast to Kamchatka on the southwest. Traveling mostly by dog sled, Bogoras was on the move for the rest of his 12 1/2 months in northeastern Asia. The journey was an ordeal. He became so ill with influenza that his Cossack companion asked where to deliver his body and papers in case he died en route. While her husband traveled, Sofia Constantinovna Bogoras stayed on the Anadyr, moving between Mariinsky Post and Markovo. She gathered the greater part of the collections for the American Museum.

While the Bogorases were occupied with the Chukchi and the Siberian Eskimo, the Jochelsons studied the Koryak, Yukaghir, and Sakha. On August 16, 1900, they arrived in Kushka, a small village at the mouth of the Gizhiga River. No Koryak were to be found. A measles epidemic during the preceding winter had killed 179 persons out of a population of 500 at the nearby village of Gizhiga, and the Reindeer Koryak had moved far into the mountains to escape the epidemic. The Jochelsons then decided to try to reach the villages of the Maritime Koryak on Penzhina Bay on horseback. The party averaged only ten miles a day

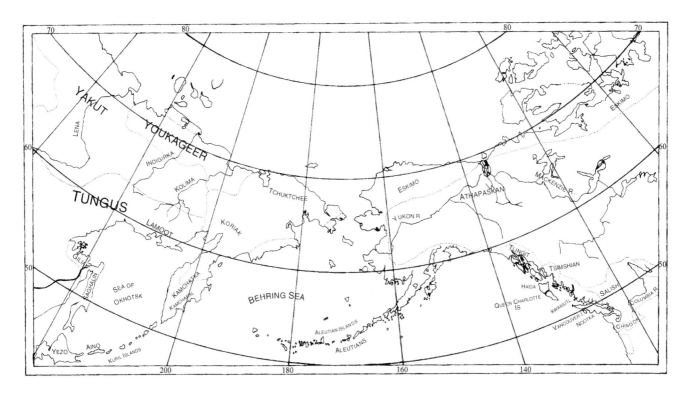

"Location of the Tribes Inhabiting the Coasts of the North Pacific Ocean" (from an early Jesup Expedition publication)

as horses became mired in boggy tundra and time was lost in extricating them. The Jochelson party finally reached the villages of the Maritime Koryak, where they spent the first half of the winter of 1900–01, living most of the time in native underground dwellings. Jochelson reported to Boas:

It is almost impossible to describe the squalor of these dwellings. The smoke, which fills the hut, makes the eyes smart. . . . Walls, ladder and household utensils are covered with a greasy soot. . . . The odor of blubber and of refuse is almost intolerable; and the inmates, intoxicated with fly agaric, add to the discomfort of the situation. The natives are infested with lice. As long as we remained in these dwellings we could not escape these insects, which we dreaded more than any of the privations of our journey. (Boas 1903: 104)

The late summer trip (August 15 to October 9, 1901) from Kushka to Verkhne-Kolymsk gives an idea of the great difficulties of traveling in Siberia. Jochelson reported:

This journey was the most difficult one that it was ever my fate to undertake. Bogs, mountain torrents, rocky passes and thick

forests combined to hinder our progress. . . . A heavy rain . . . caused the provisions to rot. Therefore we had to cut down our rations from the very beginning. After crossing the [mountain] passes . . . we reached the upper courses of the Korkodon River. By this time our horses were exhausted, and it was necessary to take a long rest. (Boas 1903: 107)

The temperature was dropping daily, and the Jochelsons knew that they would have to hurry to reach Verkhne-Kolymsk before the river froze. They spent a day building a raft and prepared to float down the Korkodon River to a Yukaghir camp where they could obtain a boat. Their guides said that the descent could be made in two days, so they left most of their food with three Sakhas who stayed with the horses and reduced their own allowance to a three-day supply. The journey, impeded by numerous rapids, rocky banks, and jams of driftwood, took nine days; for the last six, each person received only two cups of flour daily and a little tea without sugar. The party then spent four days among the Yukaghir of the Korkodon before setting

"My journey with a float of wood." The Jochelsons and their party, Korkodon River, 1901. (4194)

out in a boat for Verkhne-Kolymsk. The river froze when they were forty miles from the settlement so they had to walk two days to reach it.

Despite the difficulties posed by climate, geography, and bureaucracy, the Bogorases and the Jochelsons achieved scientific results that by any measure are extraordinary, moving Boas to write to Jesup, "You will appreciate how difficult the work of both Mr. Bogoras and Mr. Jochelson was made by these secret orders; and the full success of their investigation deserves, for this reason, the highest praise" (AMNH, Boas to Jesup, March 4, 1903). After receiving Boas's letter, Jesup wrote a note (AMNH, April 17, 1903) to the

Grand Duke Constantin, "to repeat my expression of gratitude to the Imperial Academy of Sciences."

Bogoras's work for the Jesup Expedition resulted in seven monographs, most prominently on the Chukchi. He and Sofia Bogoras collected ethnographic data, linguistic notes and 150 texts, 4,500 ethnographic artifacts, skeletal material, plaster casts of faces, archaeological specimens, 95 phonographic records, and somatological measurements of 860 individuals. No modern anthropological couple has collected such a diversity of data.

Eventually Bogoras settled in Russia and lived there the rest of his life, engaged in scientific and literary work.

After the October Revolution, he became director of the Institute of the Peoples of the North, an agency concerned with education and developmental work among the northern tribes of Siberia. In 1932, he created the Museum of the History of Religion of the Russian Academy of Sciences and was its first director.

The Jochelsons made comprehensive studies of the Koryak and Yukaghir. They collected about 4,400 ethnographic artifacts, 41 casts of faces, measurements of 900 individuals, 1,200 photographs, phonographic cylinders, skulls and archaeological specimens, and a small zoological collection. Jochelson published several monographs on the Koryak, Yukaghir, and Sakha (Yakut) and also issued his useful handbook *Peoples of Asiatic Russia* (1928). Dina Lazareevna Jochelson-Brodskaya, later to take a degree in medicine, handled all the anthropometric and medical work and most of the photography. She used some of her anthropological measurements for her doctoral dissertation at the University of Zurich, which was later published. She also published a work on the women of northeastern Siberia.

After the Jesup Expedition, Jochelson led the Aleut-Kamchatka Expedition of the Imperial Russian Geographical Society in 1909–11. From 1912 to 1922, he was division curator of the Museum of Anthropology and Ethnography of the Russian Academy of Sciences in St. Petersburg/Petrograd and collaborator of the Asiatic Museum of the Academy. From 1922 until his death in New York fifteen years later, Jochelson lived in the United States, where he was associated with the American Museum of Natural History and the Carnegie Institution of Washington.

The Jesup Expedition demonstrated the close relationship of the populations of northwestern North America and northeastern Asia and strongly supported the view that the ancestors of the American Indians came from Asia. The classic ethnographies and the irreplaceable museum collections, however, are the enduring monument of the Jesup North Pacific Expedition. This work can never be duplicated. The work of Boas and his colleagues for the expedition went a long way toward establishing their scientific reputations. Boas would train many of the leading American anthropologists of the succeeding generation, such as Ruth Benedict, A. L. Kroeber, Robert Lowie, and Margaret Mead. His style of anthropology, refined during the Jesup Expedition, dominated American anthropology for several decades.

Some scholars in Russia consider the work of Bogoras and Jochelson to be "the symbol of a new era in the ethnographic approach" and that they "have left an imposing heritage that has not yet been exhausted" (Gurvich and Kuzmina 1985:150). Nikolai Vakhtin (1994:2) writes that the Jesup Expedition "played also a very important role in shaping the Russian scholarship, namely, social anthropology, ethnology and linguistics of Siberian natives. . . . To study the history of the JNPE means, to some extent, to study the roots of the Russian Northern research." Jesup may not have been fully aware of it at his death in 1908, but he did succeed in his desire to attach his name to scientific work of major importance.

This essay has drawn heavily on our earlier publications on the Jesup Expedition (Freed, Freed, and Williamson 1988a, 1988b). Three important articles came to our attention after we published the two papers in 1988, namely Gurvich and Kuzmina (1985), Troubetzkoy (1980), and Vakhtin (1994). Information and interpretations from these articles are included in the present paper. We thank Dr. Laurel Kendall for inviting us to participate in this volume and for reading the pre-publication manuscript, and Thomas Ross Miller and Barbara Mathé for their comments on the manuscript.

Kolyma Even (Lamut) camp in snow, photographed by Waldemar Bogoras. (22460)

Drawing Shadows to Stone

Thomas Ross Miller and Barbara Mathé

THE PHOTOGRAPH is a material trace receding before our eyes. Even as we view the image of a moment long ago, the gulf of time between the pictured moment and the viewer widens. What we see today is a physical relic of what once occurred, light waves reflected off the subject striking a negative and leaving their mark. Through the veil of light and shadow captured in old photographs, we visually imagine the lives of those portrayed. The people thus glimpsed could know little of us— only that through photography, the future would try to apprehend their own lives in the past. Over time, the photograph deteriorates as emulsions fade, paper disintegrates, and glass plates crack. The integrity of the image slowly breaks up and blends into speckled shapes of black and white, the pictured subject blurring into the aging medium itself. "In a photograph," Siegfried Kracauer wrote, "a person's history is buried as if under a layer of snow" (1995:51).

Fear of the past disappearing beyond reach prompted the initiative of the Jesup North Pacific Expedition. At the end of the nineteenth century, Franz Boas and many of his fellow anthropologists believed that the indigenous cultures of the Northwest Coast of North America and of northeastern Siberia were on the verge of extinction. Traditional economies had been ruptured by colonialism, and smallpox and other diseases were rapidly decimating native populations. Many of those who survived were subject to missionary and legislative mandates that required them to forsake their traditional political systems, religious ceremonies, and livelihoods. On both sides of the north Pacific governments repressed native cultures, attempting to force people to assimilate into the dominant society. As the old customs and languages disappeared, scholars assumed that the historic identities of native peoples would vanish.

The nominal purpose of the Jesup Expedition was to reconstruct the early culture history of the northern Pacific Rim in a search for the origins of the first Americans. Boas, the chief scientist in charge of the expedition, saw an even more urgent mission in the recording and reconstruction of endangered traditional cultures. By preserving this fading past for the American Museum of Natural History, an important chapter in the history of humankind could be salvaged for the science of the future.

The members of the Jesup Expedition produced more than three thousand photographs. These pictures were part of holistic collections which aimed at representing entire cultures through myths, tales, songs, glossaries, artifacts, bones, bodily measurements, and images. The photographs include many scenes of daily and ceremonial life, demonstrations of the use of artifacts, and landscape views. By far the largest number of pictures, however, are individual portraits, taken primarily for the purpose of documenting "physical types." Subjects were shown from various angles—usually front, side-profile, and three-quarter views—in order to illustrate facial and bodily features found in the tribal populations at large. Some photographs were taken to supplement measurements and casts of the same individual. Combined with any bones and skulls that could be acquired from the same geographic locale, the physical-type photographs, measurements, and casts were meant to form a biological data bank for the history of human evolution, migration, and diffusion.

The Indians of British Columbia and Washington State were thought to be closely related to the peoples of Kamchatka and the extreme northeast of Siberia. Eskimos, according to this hypothesis, were later migrants from the eastern Arctic to Alaska. Their presence formed a sociolinguistic and genetic barrier between the Indians and the north Asian populations. Because museums already possessed excellent Bering Sea Eskimo collections made by E. W. Nelson, and Lieutenant George T. Emmons had already studied the Tlingit for the American Museum of Natural History, the Jesup project skipped over Alaskan territory (see Fitzhugh and Kaplan 1982; Emmons 1991). The Sakha (Yakut), a Turkic people whose ancestors had migrated from the southwest to northeastern Siberia, did not exactly fit the anthropological profile of an indigenous north Pacific people.* They were studied because of their influence on other peoples in the area and because Jochelson's contacts in Yakutsk offered the Museum a rare opportunity to acquire a Sakha collection.

The transformation worked by the camera on a person's image is a metaphoric model of the ethnographic enterprise at the heart of the Jesup North Pacific Expedition: to record and preserve cultures in the form of representations. Drawing shadows to stone, photography recorded a person's momentary shape in a static medium,

* Several native groups formerly known by colonial names today increasingly prefer to use their own names for themselves. We have chosen to follow their preference, except in direct quotations from historical sources. The groups referred to here (with the names by which they were formerly known in parentheses) are: Even (Lamut), Evenk (Tungus), Itel'men (Kamchadal), Kwakw<u>a</u>ka'wakw (Kwakiutl), Nanai (Gold), Nlaka'pamux (Thompson Indians), Nuxalk (Bella Coola), Sakha (Yakut) and X'muzk'i'um (Musqueam).

flattening dimensions and freezing images of the living into inert objects. The camera had the power to stop time, capture the image of a person or a landscape, embody it, miniaturize it, preserve it, reproduce it, and make it portable. Like material artifacts, people's likenesses could then be contained, transported, copied, or broken. The medium of the photograph compressed them into a form that could be carried to the archive, to be preserved in albums and plates.

The photographic trace, recording the shapes and forms of a momentary reality, is itself shaped by a process of staging and selection. The photographer chooses images and objects to represent, discarding other possibilities along the way. What made an object or an image suitably "ethnographic" was not its mere presence at the field site—for the anthropologist and other western incursions were equally present—but its identification by the anthropologist as belonging to the vital or traditional repertoire of a people. When choosing objects for ethnological collections, early anthropologists often tried to approximate an imagined ideal specimen. Just as the collector of stamps, seashells, or baseball cards considers both the singular and representative qualities of an individual piece while striving to attain

Sakha girls photographed in front of backdrop. (22172)

Case representing uses of cedar, Hall of North West Coast Indians, American Museum of Natural History, about 1902. (351)

overall completeness, museum anthropologists looked for objects and images that could illustrate whole classes of cultural phenomena. Measurement, classification, and display translated realities into the scheme of things as represented within the museum walls. Even the one-of-a-kind object could be seen as the exception that proved the rule, anomalous relative to the conceptual type from which it diverged. Yet for all its power to capture detail and represent reality, the photographic image—a unique impression of a single

moment in time from a single vantage point in space—resists this urge to idealize the particular.

The individual image pressed into the service of classification is a fitting model of the culture concept in anthropology. Boas was the first regularly to use the term "cultures" in the plural form to refer to distinct groups of people, rather than the singular "culture" to apply broadly to all of human society (Stocking 1968:203). In the object-oriented Boasian method, specific details concerning the lives of a people are highlighted—necessarily abstracted into idealized examples of their culture—when represented in a museum. Whether these imagined ideals belong more to the thoughts of the people represented than to the imagination of the anthropologist who interprets their culture is a variable expression occurring when science confronts and attempts to explain its object.

As a mode of perceptual organization, natural history orders the world into taxonomic sequences and hierarchies. If the collections narrate the past, their history also becomes that of the museum itself, inscribed with artifacts, images, and bones. Photography provided a powerful tool for ethnographic salvage, typological classification, and visual display. Like the art of memory, reading museum collections consists, in part, of re-collecting and rearranging these fragments of lived experience into a meaningful order (see Mathé 1996). The collection tells a story, but its narrative possibilities are open-ended; a different version can be constructed by rearranging objects in a cabinet, reordering classifications, or substituting one item for another. The museum is a vast repository of the shards of history, fragments of a whole whose reconstruction is an interpretive gesture. This giant memory box contains the hidden and revealed narratives embedded in collected objects and images.

Photographic visions of a traditional past are in fact signs of the modernity that both threatens and seeks to encapsulate it. A sense of urgency and loss, which has indeed been found throughout western history, was acutely felt at the turn of the century. Notions of vanishing past identities trailed in the wake of colonialism, the displacement of prior economic systems, and technology itself. If modernity meant vanishing traditions, it also brought the means to record them for posterity. The acceleration of technological change, and of the acculturation that threatened traditions, provoked the impulse to salvage. Even as the old ways disappeared, visual fragments, reconstructed and encoded in pictures, shaped the western imagination of a traditional tribal past. In this sense, the fascination with salvage and the search for origins can be seen as artifacts of a moment in western history, the nostalgia at the dawn of the twentieth century for a simpler time. Images of an indigenous past became elements in a mythical dreamscape of global

proportions, the house of the dead, the memory box of the museum.

In January 1886, Franz Boas had his first direct encounter with Northwest Coast Indians. He was working as a museum assistant, attempting to classify the disorganized American collections in Adolf Bastian's Museum für Völkerkunde in Berlin, when Captain J. Adrian Jacobsen brought a group of Nuxalk (Bella Coola) dancers and a small artifact collection to Germany in the course of a European tour. In an article on their performances and exhibitions for the *Berliner Tageblatt* (January 25, 1886), Boas warned that "with unbelievable rapidity the unique culture of this people will be displaced by the pressure of civilization, and it is to be feared that in a very short time nothing of it will remain" (Cole 1982:122). The tribes of British Columbia would become the primary focus of Boas's ethnological work for the next half-century. His earliest known field photography in the region came in 1894, when he was contracted to produce life-sized models for exhibits of native people for the U.S. National Museum (Smithsonian Institution) and the American Museum of Natural History. Working with Oregon Columbia (O. C.) Hastings, a professional photographer from Victoria, Boas directed the composition of photographic scenes with Hastings as cameraman (Jacknis 1984:10). Boas's later fieldwork on the Jesup Expedition continued and expanded on his prior research in the area.

A firm believer in the use of technology to record data, Boas equipped his team of anthropologists with cameras, photographic supplies, and recording phonographs. The collection of photographs was designed to form a cumulative body of data whose parts could be compared to each other. Although some subjects were clearly posed as models for museum mannequins and some pictures intended as plates for publication, the primary means of viewing photographic collections at the time was the album. The juxtaposition of images in the pages of albums was the most immediately accessible and comprehensive vehicle for display and study. Some albums were organized according to narrative principles, while others contained images in apparently haphazard arrangements.

The album was also a key concept in Russian photography. The standard series of "views and types," a collection of folk and ethnographic portraits, was the dominant forum for publication and display. In 1872, the Russian Geographical Society laid down guidelines for physiognomic and ethnographic photography. Full-face, profile, and full-length portraits were to be taken for purposes of anatomical study. Ethnographic photographs, influenced by painters who portrayed peasant and daily life, allowed the photographer

Photo scrapbook in Special Collections, Department of Library Services, American Museum of Natural History. Photograph by J. Beckett.

more artistic latitude to focus on costumes, faces, and "scenes from public life." In the same year, an album by Mikhail Bukhar appeared with watercolor-tinted figures and complex painted backgrounds (Barkhatova 1992:41–50). This move toward pictorial simulation of context parallelled the museum diorama techniques that artists and preparators at the American Museum of Natural History would later independently develop. Retouching a photograph by adding a painted background acknowledges the isolation of the subject from its actual context. As in a diorama, the artist may try to reconstruct an imagined setting. In each case, representational media are combined to create an environmental illusion.

During the 1890s, ethnographic photography flourished throughout the Russian empire as newly formed photographic societies debated the artistic versus documentary

merits of the camera. The Jesup Expedition photographs made by the Russian anthropologists Waldemar Bogoras, Dina Jochelson-Brodskaya, and Waldemar Jochelson include relatively formal portraits as well as casual snapshots of their native subjects, many of whom had long been acquainted with Jochelson and Bogoras during their exile in the area.

The small tribes of the north were undergoing cataclysmic demographic shifts (Krupnik 1993; Slezkine 1994). The Yukaghir population, for example, once numerous, had fallen precipitously to a nadir of some two hundred souls. (In the late 1990s they number around one thousand.) During the Jesup period, smallpox was ravaging the surviving groups of nomadic Yukaghir. Because of the epidemic the anthropologists met far fewer natives than they had anticipated. Jochelson wrote to Boas,

There are fewer measurements of the Yukaghir than the Koryak. There are so few Yukaghir in the first place, they are dispersed and move continuously so that the ethnologist in this polar country must be in constant search of them. Often we had to cover great distances just to get from one camp to the next. It often happened that we didn't find the tents at the specified location any more. However, every nomadic Yukaghir or Tungus we met, was held, measured, photographed and questioned. (DA)

On the Northwest Coast, native survival faced comparable threats. The Kwakwaka'wakw (Kwakiutl) were ravaged by pneumonia, influenza and other diseases, and their numbers declined between 1883 and 1905 from about 2,300 people to only about 1,300 (Cole and Chaikin 1990:70–71, 96). Other tribes, including the Haida, Tsimshian, and Nlaka'pamux (Thompson), were being rapidly assimilated into the mainstream of Canadian society, thanks to missionaries, governmental policies, and socioeconomic changes. Facing what appeared to be the imminent loss of whole tribes, salvage anthropologists recorded the moment and reconstructed earlier traditions, collecting those objects of native manufacture and use which they thought would soon be archaic.

In Siberia Bogoras and Jochelson, collecting cultural

fragments which they didn't expect to survive, recorded shamans' songs and acquired shamans' coats, hats, and drums for the collection. They also photographed some of the costumes being worn, carefully posed against backdrops. These pictures were apparently meant to serve as models for museum mannequins (see plates 17, 54, and 55). The project of representation was premised on the absence of a living tradition, if not now then in the future. The photographs demonstrating the use of the collected objects also documented the retirement of the shamans' dress and paraphernalia from ceremonial practice, and their transfer to the museum collection. The ritual of the camera recorded the desacralization of these shamanic garments in the moment of their transformation from vestments of living power to inert artifacts for collection, study, and display. For the collected objects, the camera was indeed witnessing a last performance.

Ironically, in "salvaging" items for museums, anthropologists also hastened the demise of the very things they sought to preserve. On the one hand, the collected traditional objects were "rescued" just before the encroaching progress of the twentieth century rendered them obsolete; but on the other hand, the intrusion of the modern science of collecting made their removal more complete. Although the loss of traditions prophesied by anthropology thus became to some extent a self-fulfilling prophecy, the traditions were not necessarily lost beyond recovery. Today, as deeply rooted cultural forms and the native identities they express reemerge, artists and others who have kept traditions alive are studying the objects and images preserved in museums. One hundred years after the Jesup Expedition, the ethnographic collections and archives remain a valuable guide to cultural revival.

Unlike memory, which frames meaningful events, photography preserves only the material facts of a particular place at a moment in time. As photographic images age, their context gradually disappears; when the original referent no longer exists, the antiquated image becomes detached from the world that gave it meaning. The image of the obsolete is cast adrift in a sea of time. The material trace of the photograph is the residue of history. Archival fragments evoke the disintegrated unity from which they were cut. As pieces in a collection, they are jumbled and rearranged in archives, albums, books, databases, and exhibitions. Large collections of images are intended to be sorted, edited, and displayed in various media.

When photographs are gathered together in an archive, Kracauer observed, the simultaneity of multiple perspectives removes them further from human experience. "Their original order is lost; they no longer cling to the spatial context that linked them with an original out of which the memory image was selected." Their reassemblage in various combinations is "reminiscent of *dreams* in which the fragments of daily life become jumbled. This game shows that the valid organization of things remains unknown" (Kracauer 1995:63). If multiple perspectives, sequences, and relationships are possible, there can be no single definitive ordering or classification. The unending possibilities for the juxtaposition of images, outside the linear time in which they were conceived, reveals the arbitrariness of the entire project to collect and represent whole cultures.

The origins of natural history museums can be traced to European "cabinets of curiosities." Historically, the cabinet was a room filled with an odd assortment of unusual natural and manufactured objects gathered from near and far. Within the boundaries of the chamber, fragments of nature and culture were isolated and contained. The camera, a box of another sort, also isolates and contains images. Both museum walls and photographic frame separate the image from its environment, boxing it for preservation and analysis. Like an object in a museum, an image captured by the camera has a "second life." Removed from its original context, the collected image represents the world from which it came and takes on new meaning in relation to other, disparate images.

The optical principle on which the photographic process is based occurs in the *camera obscura,* when light passes through a pinhole in the wall of a darkened room to create an inverse projection on the opposite wall. To expand the range of the camera, the room became a portable, miniature box. Bound to a fixed perspective, the apparatus captures reflections of the world outside the chamber. The two-dimensional picture bears the authoritative stamp of truth, but is blind to what existed just outside the frame.

The allegory of the cave in Plato's *Republic* describes what happens when images, isolated from context, are framed in a fixed perspective. Plato's cave of illusions is a box with a single opening, through which the shadows of the outside world are cast. The people in the cave are prisoners, bound in a fixed position so they can see only the wall before them, not the opening above and behind. Along a road between the prisoners and the opening, people carry statues and objects, but the bound prisoners can perceive only their shadows and echoes. The cave-dwellers take the shadows to be the reality of the outside world, for they know nothing else.

The camera resembles Plato's cave. Unable to travel to distant lands or go back in time, the viewer of a photograph sees only a shadow of what once was, flat and in distorted perspective. Yet, the limitations of a single vantage point can be partially overcome by picturing a subject from several angles in succession. For Boas, the scientific utility of physical-type images was constrained by the two-dimensional medium (Jacknis 1984:45). To compensate for the singular point of view, the limited field of vision, and the single moment of exposure, photographers could picture an individual from several angles.

Physical anthropology was central to the early discipline and to the Bering Strait migration hypothesis in particular. Classification and typology of physical traits provided a way to reconstruct the natural history of native peoples. Anthropometry, the measuring of the human body and its parts, was useful mainly for its comparative data. In contrast to earlier evolutionary and diffusionist models, independent but interrelated data on race, language, and

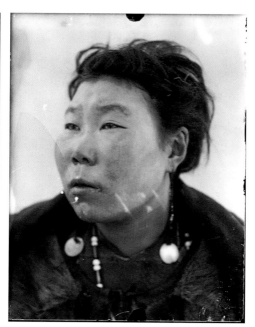

Sakha man, front view and profile. (21198 and 21199)   *Yukaghir woman, three-quarter view. (21147)*

culture formed the cornerstones of Boas's historical anthropology. It was Boas's contention that measurements could be meaningful only if an individual were assigned to the correct ideal type, based on very large cumulative samples, against which his or her features could be compared.

Even as Boas gathered data for the study of physical types, his work did much to destabilize the concept of fixed racial characteristics. The classical methods used by physical anthropologists emphasized the shape of the head as measured by the cephalic index, the ratio of the maximum width of the head to its maximum length. Standard methodology was premised on the numerical average representing an ideal type, but Boas argued that samples included individuals with deformities and other peculiarities. The average, then, was not a truly "ideal" type but in many ways a statistical accident. Before Boas, scientists also ignored a person's growth and development when interpreting physical measurements. Boas acknowledged that an individual's headform and body measurements change over the course of a lifetime. In an 1899 article, "Some Recent Criticisms of Physical Anthropology," he cautioned that classification of individuals by type could not be as definite

or detailed as classification by language. Instead, he claimed that statistical analysis would reveal the data on race, language, and culture as independent but interrelated (Boas 1940:165–71).

Throughout his career, from his early work with Eskimos in Baffin Land to his prominent role in later public debates on immigration and miscegenation, Boas's scrupulous scientific methods confirmed his relativistic views of human equality. Carefully drawn comparative analyses repeatedly exposed as a myth the alleged innate superiority of one group over another.

Boas's techniques were not widely accepted right away. Classifying populations by physical type, like accurately describing languages and cultures, first required comprehensive collections of data as evidence. Measurement was adopted as a method precisely because local and individual variants were so minute as to evade descriptive analysis. The problem of reconstructing the early history of humankind made skulls—which could rarely be obtained without difficulty, if at all—of enormous collection value. Actual bones were the most reliable and scientifically useful acquisitions, followed in importance by casts, measurements, and photographs, in that order. Like measurements, photographs were intended to supplement verbal descriptions, not to serve as primary data.

Making casts in the field was difficult for the anthropologists and may have been frightening for some subjects, although some people came willingly to have their casts taken in exchange for payment. A cast was made by covering the face with plaster of Paris to make a mold, from which a copy of facial features could be reproduced in plaster or metal. This technique was similar to that used in producing metal duplicates of relief surfaces, impressions known as "stereotypes." Casts were used for statistical analysis and as models for busts and the heads of museum mannequins. Through the art and science of museum representation, the faces of individuals became stereotypical, idealized images of racially and culturally classified groups.

Dina Jochelson-Brodskaya measured 720 Koryak, Evenk (Tungus), and Sakha men, women, and children. In addition, she produced special measurements of more than 120 Evenk, Sakha, and Yukaghir women. These measurements formed the basis of her doctoral dissertation under Rudolph Martin in Zurich. In a 1907 article for *Russkii Antropologischeskii Zhurnal,* she described taking measurements in the field:

My husband and I, our interpreter, and other assistants had to produce different works at the same time in our own small canvas tent, heated by a little iron stove. Under such conditions I found it impossible to produce special measurements of Koryak women. . . .

We spent the winter of 1901–02 in the region of the Kolyma River, where I measured the Yukaghir and some of the Yakuts. The Yukaghir are even more bashful than the Tungus; but, thanks to

Bust of Koryak man. (12789)

Photograph illustrating the method of making duplicate busts. (33635)

Informant demonstrating cedar-spinning for life group shown on page 21; George Hunt on right, Franz Boas on left. (11608)

their peaceful disposition and trust in my husband, who had lived a long time in their midst in the capacity of a member of the Yakut Expedition (1895–1897), they willingly came to me to be measured. I produced the measurements of Yukaghir women in their winter lodgings—simple wooden frames. I situated myself with the women being measured in front of a light hanging curtain, and on the other side of the curtain stood our interpreter, the Yukaghir Alexei Dolganov, translating everything that I said for them. In his presence the Yukaghir women worried that there might be some cracks between the curtain and the adjacent wall.

Jochelson-Brodskaya's methods appear consistent with Boas's, emphasizing not only the cephalic index but also the growth of an individual in determining a person's classificatory type. She concluded that the Chukchi, who lived closest to the American Indians, resembled them in growth and head width. The growth of Asiatic Eskimos was less than that of Alaskan Eskimos but more than that of the Chukchi, while their cephalic indices were nearly equal to those of Alaskan Eskimos. These findings appear to support Boas's and Bogoras's hypothesis that Northwest Coast Indians are close relatives of the Chukchi, Koryak, Itel'men (Kamchadal), and Yukaghir, and that the Eskimos had arrived from the east to drive a wedge between them (see Freed, Freed, and Williamson 1988a and 1988b).

While Boas's representational methodology made museum collecting into a science of measurement for the taxonomic purpose of racial typology, it also ascribed a high moral purpose to the scientific impulse of salvage. The photographers enlisted native subjects to dramatize the earlier, more traditional cultures that were held to be vanishing throughout the north Pacific. In making their collections for the museum, the members of the Jesup Expedition tended to privilege signs of indigenous identity over the telltale hybrid, at times editing out coloniality and a certain degree of individuality in the composition of photographs. Boas's own method of photography in the field involved staging scenes, in collaboration with Indians, to portray the precontact past. But Boas occasionally pulled the camera back to playfully reveal his own fakery. In the 1894 shot demonstrating the spinning of cedar for an American Museum of Natural History model (facing page), Boas and his principal collaborator, Hunt, can be seen holding a backdrop that isolates the figure and conceals a Canadian picket fence. In this case, by documenting his own process of scientific documentation, Boas ensured that later generations would be able to separate the reconstruction from the reality. In analogous fashion, modern artifact conservation employs techniques that make the repairs to restored objects hardly noticeable in display but evident to the trained eye so that future generations will be able to distinguish the original parts from later museological interventions.

Cropped, retouched, deteriorating, or degraded photographs partially erase history by effacing memory. The passage of time sets in motion a continual process of remembering and forgetting, obscuring and reinscribing the past. Each picture casts a unique light on the hidden and revealed structure of events. In Milan Kundera's novel *The Book of Laughter and Forgetting* (1981), a Czechoslovakian official who falls from grace is airbrushed out of an historical photograph of the regime he had served. But as it turns out, on the cold winter's day when the photograph was first taken, the doomed man had placed his hat on the leader's head. This hat remains behind in the retouched photograph, symbolizing (for those who can decode the image) the hidden story that runs parallel to the official version of events. Archival photographs, careful constructions that capture the spark of the accidental, play the narrative role of lingering memories in a fading history. What sorts of evidence might they provide, and how might we interpret them? (See Miller 1992.)

The task of reconstruction and representation in the field sometimes demanded a sophisticated level of artifice. It was especially challenging in the north Pacific, where intercultural contact had a long history. The ethnographers could not avoid some obvious signs of acculturation, nor did they wish to in all cases. Boasian methods of reenacting precontact traditions were more applicable to the nomadic hunter-gatherers of the tundra than they were to people in large towns, where native people had lived for centuries mixed with settler populations. The complete filtration of foreign influences out of the collections would have presented unacceptable levels of distortion. If anthropology, driven by racial typology and the ethos of the salvage imperative, still framed its subject proper as the strictly indigenous, the Jesup Expedition, with assistance from native ethnographers like George Hunt, was able to stretch its boundaries to convey a more accurate impression of real lives.

In northeastern Siberia, the classificatory situation was murky. Old settlers, new Russian emigrants and exiles, Cossacks, and numerous native groups had long histories of intermarriage, shared economic exchange, and Orthodox Christianity mingled with shamanism. The Jochelsons and Bogorases documented the Russian exile communities in Siberia, of which they were a part, as well as the tribal peoples they were assigned to study. In areas with heavily Russianized populations, they turned to the detailed study of acculturation. Unable to travel in the most extreme weather conditions, the expedition parties were forced to spend a whole winter in the Russian post of Markovo. Taking advantage of the long wait, Bogoras and Jochelson made artifact collections from so-called Russianized natives and other groups whom they classified by various terms denoting hybridity. Signs of acculturation are most evident in photographs taken in and around Yakutsk, the imperial

Blankets piled on beach at Fort Rupert potlatch, with speaker in middle. (42967)

headquarters for the collection of fur tribute for nearly three hundred years.

Certain trade items of western manufacture were at that time thoroughly enmeshed in Northwest Coast Indian cultures. For nearly fifty years, since the founding of the Hudson's Bay post at Fort Rupert in 1849, Hudson's Bay Company blankets had been given away in large numbers at ceremonial potlatches, along with the blankets of native manufacture used in earlier times. They were an import so fully adapted and integrated that they could hardly have been ignored or explained away (see plate 8). At Fort Rupert in 1894, Boas and Hastings had photographed Kwakwa̱ka̱'wakw dressed in their normal western-style clothing. Because it was the winter ceremonial season, however, many Kwakwa̱ka̱'wakw also wore or held traditional signs of ritual status such as a headpiece, cedar bark ring, or copper (see plate 24).

On the Skeena River in August 1897, Boas and the archaeologist Harlan Smith took a series of physical shots aboard the steamer *Danube*. They spent much of the trip in the company of gold-rush prospectors on the way to Alaska (see Rohner 1969:228–32). Missions were well established at Skidegate and Massett on the Queen Charlotte Islands, and the great majority of Haida and Tsimshian were already thoroughly Christianized. Among the people in the

Potlatch participants counting blankets at Fort Rupert.
(411785)

portraits is Anna McKay, wearing a Salvation Army pin
(plate 26). Louisa and her husband Samuel of Massett were
paid $1.00 apiece for cast and photos. Louisa is one of sev-
eral women in this series wearing a blanket, a sign of status
(plates 28 and 29). Beside the typical right and left profiles
of Louisa, an unidentified man in a trilby hat grins, out
of focus, in the background of plate 29. In plate 28, for
unknown reasons, the man's blurry image was later partially
effaced. This curious retouching of the photograph is
apparently a botched attempt to remove obvious signs of
acculturation from the scene. The more westernized figure

has been placed under erasure, leaving Louisa, wrapped
up in her Indian blanket, alone; but the trace of his form
remains as a gap in the picture and a question mark in
its possible narratives.

After a few days on the S.S. *Danube,* Boas and Smith
found that many Indians had left the area. Smith, with
nothing left to do, traveled with the camera to Bella Bella,
then on to Rivers Inlet. Boas remained behind at Port
Essington, commissioning paintings of faces from a Haida
artist and hoping to take more casts and measurements
of Tsimshian women. (When two women appeared wanting
their faces cast, Boas was annoyed that he was unable to
photograph them [Rohner 1969:228–32]). Meanwhile,
Harlan Smith continued to accumulate physical-type pic-

Sakha mother and daughter in Russian overcoats and felt hats. (1771 and 1772)

tures. In Bella Bella he photographed Jack Tsacoola wearing a kerchief tied in a distinctive circular form virtually identical to that of a traditional cedar bark neck ring (plate 25). Bark rings were worn in rituals as a mark of initiation, despite the provincial government's attempts to suppress the ceremonial use of cedar bark. The portrait of Jack Tsacoola thus may be read as evidence of both dynamic cultural transformation and the unbroken expression of Indian identity, simultaneously embodied by the ring in his trade-cloth kerchief. Interpreting the photograph today, Jack Tsacoola's neck ring is at once an emblem of tradition and a sign of modernity. Like Kundera's hat, it symbolizes both memory and loss.

This doubleness situates the ethnographic scene as a transitional moment in history. Yet it was the intervention of salvage anthropology itself, with the camera present to bear witness, that defined such moments as poised on the boundary between visions of a traditional past and an assimilated future. Reexamining the images one hundred years later, an ethnographic moment may appear quite differently as a temporary adaptation, an historical anomaly, or a passing style.

Although many native peoples on both sides of the Bering Strait had seen cameras and photographs before, some responded with ingenious curiosity. At Fort Rupert in 1894, Boas had observed:

The people are curious to see the pictures from the back of the camera. I was just about to photograph a woman when somebody noticed that the picture [i.e., the ground-glass image, which appears inverted] was upside down, and he ran away telling every-body that her clothes had fallen over her head (Rohner 1969:189).

Some people, like the nomadic Yukaghir, had never seen a camera before. Their name for the apparatus, "the three-legged device that draws a person's shadow to stone," accu-rately described the Jochelsons' light-sensitive glass-plate camera mounted on its tripod.

The Jochelsons often set up two tents in the field, one for their living quarters and the other to serve as a portable photo studio and darkroom (see plate 2). During the cold-est months of the Siberian winter, traveling by dogsled with Maritime Koryaks, they could take no pictures because the equipment was frozen (see plate 40). The photographers on the Northwest Coast also developed their pictures in the field. Weather conditions there were far less of an obstacle than in Siberia, especially since the anthropologists traveled for shorter periods and in the summer.

The bulky photographic equipment, added to the already immense burden of supplies and collections carried on the expedition, was difficult to transport and set up. The cameras used on the Jesup Expedition were unwieldy con-traptions, requiring the use of tripods and a separate glass plate for each exposure. Although the hand-held box cam-era had been in use since the early 1890s, the expedition members followed the lead of most professional photogra-phers of the day in opting for large-format view cameras instead. The latter were capable of producing greater detail and a finer image than were the smaller Kodaks used by amateurs. The slow film and large format required either strong lighting or slow shutter speeds to obtain correct exposures in the northern and typically grey regions of the expedition. Most of the photographs were taken outdoors, where even in scarce sunlight it would be possible to make an exposure without flash powder. Some interior shots were very likely lit artificially, adding the burden of explosive flash powder, which had to be kept cool and dry, to the already difficult load. Native architecture and practices did allow for occasional indoor photography with apparently natural light. The smoke holes in houses in Siberia, and the habit on the Northwest Coast of moving roof planks from winter houses to summer villages, sometimes allowed sun-light to pass through and illuminate interiors (Jonaitis 1991:76).

Spontaneous or candid snapshots were usually impos-sible with a large-format camera mounted on a tripod, requiring a complicated routine to make an exposure. After choosing the site of the picture and setting the camera in place, the photographer framed and focused the image through the ground glass at the back of the camera. He or she had to disappear under a light-proof black cloth in order to see the image clearly in the glass. Once the image was set, the photographer emerged from under cover, closed the lens, set the shutter, and slid the holder with the glass negative into the rear of the camera. The shutter was cocked and the slide in front of the film pulled out. Finally, the exposure was made at the moment the shutter was . released, probably by means of a short cable. The elaborate preparations, long still poses, and sudden exposures made for some uncomfortable situations in the field. Jochelson wrote that he "had to refrain from photographing nervous persons" (1926:35–36). One Yukaghir woman fell victim to a fit of Arctic hysteria, a syndrome of temporary madness, set off by the crack of the shutter of Jochelson's camera (see Mathé and Miller 1997).

Having established the frame, it was only at the point of standing next to the camera and holding the release that the photographer could choose the precise moment to be exposed. Even outdoors, under the maximum possible exposure for a cloudy day, images would blur when the photographer tried to photograph a fast-moving subject. Occasionally, attempts to capture movement in low light or with flash powder were re-shot several times with blurred or badly exposed results. Some of these images were eventu-ally published in the expedition memoir series as simplified line drawings based on the failed exposures. Such persis-tence on the part of the anthropologists suggests that, from the start, these particular scenes—often illustrating functional processes such as making fire—were composed with publication in mind.

The inability of a single photograph to capture sustained activity over a period of time could be somewhat compensated for by arranging a series of images, which together might form a narrative of an event. Harlan Smith, who meticulously recorded sets of images to illustrate temporal or developmental sequences, presaged later "cinematic" approaches to photography (Morris 1994:66–76). Picturing the passage of time, Smith shot a series of a shell heap he was digging, showing the archaeological evidence uncovered at various stages of the excavation. Margaret Blackman (1981:3, 48) has described anthropological photography as a form of visual archaeology, revealing change over time through successive images. The combination of photographs made in the same place years apart illustrates history in stages. Smith's work, however, documents changes occurring not over a period of years but from moment to moment, capturing a single chain of events in a series of images to show processes not revealed in a single still photograph.

At Fort Rupert in June of 1898, Smith exposed a series of images that included rare photographs of a Kwakwaka'wakw potlatch. A potlatch is a celebratory feast at which large quantities of goods, measuring and reflecting the wealth and status of the host, are given away to invited guests. The chief's largesse bears testimony to his greatness and social rank. In order to assert their own status, other high-ranking chiefs must reciprocate with other potlatches at a later date, attempting to outdo the generosity of previous hosts. Through this ceremonial system of mutual exchange, goods were distributed throughout communities and rank was established and maintained. Seasonal potlatches were held to mark a variety of ritual and other important occasions.

A fixed location at a suitable distance was necessary to capture the scene in a panoramic sequence. With assistance from the Kwakwaka'wakw George Hunt, Harlan Smith could anticipate the events of the potlatch and was able to set up his camera in a location from which he could most effectively record it as it happened. A second set of unidentified photographs from Fort Rupert appears to have been taken by O. C. Hastings at the same potlatch. When combined, the images from the two sets show the progression of the event. They depict a fire being prepared on the beach to welcome the guests, others awaiting their arrival, then the visitors coming ashore with the chief, followed by the display and counting of blankets. The key to linking the two series is a pair of photographs of the same event, men gambling on the beach, taken in two different formats. One (plate 46), credited to Smith, is in the six-by-eight format he generally used. The other (plate 47) is from the unidentified series. Two boys, one wearing a scarf and the other a straw hat, appear at the right edge of the first photograph and the left edge of the second.

Hastings, who happened to be in Fort Rupert at the time, worked as a laborer and occasional photographer for the Jesup Expedition and could have produced the smaller images. Also passing through Fort Rupert at the time was Roland Dixon, who had been studying and photographing the Lillooet for Boas. Dixon was on his way to join psychologist Livingston Farrand, who studied and made phonograph recordings of the Quinault and Quileute for the Jesup Expedition. Dixon traveled to the Olympic Peninsula in Washington State to take physical-type photographs of those tribes.

Potlatching, then banned by the Canadian provincial governments and on the wane throughout the Northwest Coast, seemed to be a genuinely disappearing tradition. Among the Kwakwaka'wakw, however, the ceremony was actually increasing in frequency. This was partly attributable to an increase of wealth from the fur trade and canneries, along with a decrease in population. But the growth of potlatching was also a measure of the cultural tenacity of the people. Although the ban was very rarely enforced, the Kwakwaka'wakw took some risk in defying attempts by Ottawa to curb their ceremonial lives (Cole and Chaikin 1990). Boas wrote letters to newspapers and provincial

Photograph representing Koryak fire-drilling ceremony. (4124)

Drawing based on photographs of Koryak fire-drilling ceremony. (44606)

6415
4123

Photograph of Maritime Koryak village. (1574)

authorities defending the custom as the basis of a sound socioeconomic system of exchange and status. The presence of George Hunt, whose relatives were the only storeowners who publicly encouraged the holding of potlatches, and Hastings's prior experience photographing a potlatch with Boas in 1894, may have contributed to the Jesup team being allowed to photograph the proceedings freely.

In 1901, Hunt got a camera and continued to work (Jacknis 1984:8). His photographs of a later potlatch, taken from a closer vantage point than Smith's and Hastings's, were more intimate and reflect his insider's knowledge and membership in the community. Other ceremonies, such

as the *hamatsa* and the *tamananawas*—so-called cannibal dances which featured symbolic ritual cannibalism—were more difficult for anthropologists to witness. In 1900 Hunt was arrested, tried, and eventually acquitted for allegedly participating in such a ceremony; in his defense he stated that he had been present as an anthropologist, and he appealed to Boas as a character witness. His later *hamatsa* photographs, however, were evidently posed specially for the camera. (See plates 43 and 44.)

The degree to which events were staged for the anthropologists varied. In Siberia, some shamans forbade the phonograph recording of actual ceremonies, instead performing special demonstrations in front of the machine. Besides the possibility that the recordings might be used

Museum miniature based on photographs of Maritime Koryak villages. (326742)

for evil purposes, they were concerned that spirits would fly into the recording horn and be trapped irretrievably inside the phonograph box. Jochelson witnessed and photographed a *ysakh* festival, a sacred celebration of spring held annually by the Sakha. (See plates 49 and 50.) The photographs show circle dances being witnessed by crowds and imperial officials, and the serving of *kumiss,* a sacred drink of fermented mare's milk, from traditional vessels. The ceremony was actually held out of season to accommodate Jochelson's schedule (Vladimir Ivanov, pers. com.; see Jochelson 1933, Balzer 1992).

In Siberia and along the Northwest Coast, additional pictures were taken by professional photographers. Berthold Laufer's photographs of Amur River peoples were so amateurish that Boas suggested he hire a professional (Black 1988:24–30; Kendall 1988:104). (See plate 34.) There are more photographs of the Koryak in the collection than of any other Siberian group, since both Bogoras's and Jochelson's teams spent time in and around Kamchatka. In the dead of winter, photography was impossible in raging blizzards and temperatures as cold as minus 29 degrees Celsius.

American Museum of Natural History, South Facade, 1899.
(368)

Toward the end of his journey Jochelson, out of money, was forced to sell off photographic equipment and supplies to reach Yakutsk. When he finally arrived there he paid a professional photographer twenty-five rubles to continue the work.

The exchange of images worked in the opposite direction as well. The native people had to picture the museum and the people of New York before the scientists could make pictures of the natives. To explain their mission, the anthropologists carried pictures of the American Museum of Natural History. They gave these pictures to informants in order to persuade them that objects and images they contributed to the collection would reside in a regal house in a great city. Harlan Smith wrote to John H. Winser, the museum's financial officer, from the field: "Have used up all my pictures of the Museum. Could use more to advantage among people who have specimens" (DA). The process of representing others actually began, then, with natives visually imagining the museum and its public. If suitably impressed by the images from New York, they would reciprocate.

In earlier cabinets of curiosities each item, removed from its original context and assuming a new place in the arrange-

ment of the collection, was visually classified in relation to other objects by means of juxtaposition and hierarchy. The diorama, life group, and model, on the other hand, like photographic panoramas, are attempts to reconstruct original contexts in the form of museum representations, simulated pictures of distant cultural spaces. Boas, whose introduction to Northwest Coast Indians had come when the Nuxalk performed in Berlin and who had exhibited living Kwakwa̱ka̱'wakw people at the Chicago Columbian Exposition in 1893, pioneered the fabrication of visual reconstructions of cultures. Boas's museum exhibits greatly influenced the development of American anthropology, which gradually moved toward his concept of cultures. The way in which anthropologists came to focus on distinct groups can be seen in part as originating in a pictorial device.

Boas's museum exhibits displayed artifacts in the setting of other objects from the same group of people, rather than arraying them according to kind or to superficial resemblance (see Jacknis 1985). The social meaning of an object, not its outer form, determined its place in display and classification. In a series of articles published in *Science* in 1887, he debated the question of museum arrangements with Otis T. Mason and John Wesley Powell of the U.S. National Museum (Smithsonian Institution) (see Boas 1887, Mason 1887, Powell 1887; also Stocking 1974:1–20). The arrangement of Boas's exhibits for the American Museum of Natural History reflected his notions of distinct cultures and races, rather than older ideas of evolution and diffusion from centers of civilization. Objects and images were classified on the basis of *difference*—racial, artistic, historical, or linguistic—rather than by affinity, as the evolutionists had done. In another way, the physical-type photographs, taken for purposes of measurement and comparison, also throw differences in individual features into relief against the uniform white-cloth background of the standard format. Whether a photograph provides or screens out context depends in part on how closely the subject is framed and whether artificial backgrounds are used to screen out or to represent settings.

Photographs taken in the field, staged or not, were invaluable guides to the reproduction of "typical" scenes. In some cases, images from several different photographs taken in the field were combined into composite scenes for museum miniatures. One such model was built from a series of photographs taken by the Jochelsons in Maritime Koryak villages (see page 37). It remains on display in the American Museum of Natural History's Hall of Asian Peoples to represent a so-called Paleolithic environment. The real inhabitants of one village were particularly averse to being studied. Jochelson wrote to Boas on December 3, 1900:

> The natives of Kamenskoye are not as helpful as the Parenzers. They don't like to be measured, especially the women, although they are offered presents. Older people stop the younger ones from singing into the phonograph saying [that] "the old one" as they call the phonograph will take their voices and they'll die.

The Koryak explained the phonograph by saying that a small man who imitated people's voices lived inside the box. From what the ethnographers wrote, though, the typical response to the recording machines was enthusiasm and curiosity, not fear or awe (see Taussig 1993). Many Koryak enjoyed listening to the commercial wax cylinders Bogoras and Jochelson carried, and especially to their own voices played back during recording sessions. Like the phonograph, the camera was a box for reproducing sensory impressions. "In the final effect," Walter Benjamin (1977) wrote, "the mechanical methods of reproduction are a technology of miniaturization." Living, three-dimensional realities were freeze-dried into small, flat photographic images; the transformation to museum representation was completed when selected scenes were reconstituted as three-dimensional miniatures based on the field photographs.

The models in the Hall of Northwest Coast Indians, ranging from tiny to near life-sized, are copied from photographs taken during the Jesup Expedition and Boas's 1894 fieldwork. The miniature scene illustrating the daily life of the Nlaka'pamux is a composite from photographs taken at various field sites. One figure, a woman tanning a deer hide, appears in the miniature scene and again, nearly full-sized, isolated in a large display box. While the miniature zooms out to a great distance, showing the big picture on a small scale, the larger model zooms in to show figures in detail. The large-scale life group shows the woman dressed in traditional clothing, tanning a small piece of deerskin stretched on a frame. At her feet are a number of genuine artifacts, including two baskets.

The life-group model was based on a set of photographs carefully composed by Harlan Smith at Kamloops, B.C. (see plates 58 and 59). Smith acquired the actual deerskin, which was much bigger than that used in the life group, along with other artifacts. In a letter to Boas on April 27, 1898, he wrote that he had collected

> Deer skin, scraper, stone in handle—birch bark basket and stone scraper. For these last 4 I paid $4.00. This seemed high but I photoed the woman scraping skin and thought you would need a skin and scraper for the group showing squaw scraping skin. . . . and knowing you had a digging stick I only bought basket for I thought you had no old dirty used baskets and would want one for the group so not to take any out of the case collection. (DA, 1898–41)

Apart from the altered scale, the most obvious difference between the photograph and the model is the woman's clothing. The Indian photographed by Smith, like virtually all Nlaka'pamux at that time, wore western-style clothing, but the model is in traditional dress (Hill-Tout 1978). Like the other people studied by the Jesup Expedition, the Nlaka'pamux actively participated in the construction of their own museum representation by posing, selling traditional items to the museum, relating myths, songs, and stories, and recreating the remembered past.

Many of the representations that resulted from these moments of anthropological encounter were collaborative acts of theater. The production of these images resulted from complex negotiations of identity. Although some subjects were reluctant, others freely cooperated and composed scenes for the camera. Throughout his journey among the Chukchi, Koryak, and Asian Eskimo, Bogoras photographed men wearing traditional suits of armor and posing in mock battle stances (see, for example, plate 60). There is a playful attitude in these shots that suggests a good-natured game of make-believe. For the Chukchi, who successfully fought off Russian conquerors for more than 250 years, as for the other people studied, anthropological photographs dramatized a proud sovereign past. The traditions portrayed by the Jesup North Pacific Expedition were reconstructions of that past for an uncertain future.

Museum mannequin of Koryak warrior based on field photographs. (311652)

40

The Jesup Expedition Photographs

1 / In the mid-eighteenth century, the expanding Russian empire fought wars of conquest against the Koryak people of Kamchatka. The neighboring Chukchi warriors of the Chukotka Peninsula resisted invasion for another hundred years before they were finally conquered. In 1900, anthropologists for the American Museum of Natural History were still able to collect examples of the traditional chain-mail armor worn by marksmen in battle. (1559)

2 / Dina Jochelson-Brodskaya did much of the Siberian photographic work for the Jesup North Pacific Expedition. She and her husband Waldemar Jochelson, leader of the Siberian parties, often set up two tents in the field. One served as living and writing quarters, the other as portable studio and darkroom. (4148)

3 / About half the photographs from the Jesup Expedition are portraits taken primarily to document "physical types." Subjects were shown in frontal, three-quarter, and profile views depicting their facial or bodily features. Combined with bones, measurements, and casts, these pictures were meant to help determine the racial characteristics of tribal populations and trace the history of diffusion. (2270, 2271, 2272)

4 / In 1894, Franz Boas collected objects in British Columbia for museum life-group exhibits. On the occasion when this photograph was taken he wrote to his wife, "I invited everybody to an apple feast, for which they especially decked themselves out. . . . While the people were on their way to the feast we got some quick shots." (335772)

5 / Contact with Canadian traders had a lasting effect on Northwest Coast cultures. Metal tools, Hudson's Bay Company blankets, and other manufactured items were quickly absorbed into native life. Alert Bay was founded in 1870, when a salmon cannery opened seeking Indian labor. By the 1880s, western-style clothing was commonplace. (411790)

6 / This house post represents Capilano I, a Coast Salish warrior who fought the Lekwiltok Kwakwaka'wakw. Standing next to the post is his nephew's nephew Capilano III, a X'muzk'i' um (Musqueam) chief known as Charlie. Some Coast Salish carvings are more naturalistic and less stylized than the art of other Northwest Coast peoples. (411787)

7 / The Reindeer Koryak offered sacrifices to the Supreme Being and supernatural guardians; sacrifices to evil spirits were made reluctantly to protect humans. Jochelson requested that a reindeer sacrifice be posed for his camera, but was told it would be a sin. After he offered to pay two bricks of tea and two bundles of tobacco and let them keep the meat, however, the Koryak agreed. (1480)

8 / Hudson's Bay Company blankets became an integral medium of exchange in potlatch ceremonies, in addition to traditional robes and blankets of Indian manufacture. Although Canadian
laws banned potlatching, with new wealth from trade and factory-made items the period around
the turn of the century saw an efflorescence of the Kwakwa̱ka'wakw potlatch. (411813)

9 / George Hunt, a native of Fort Rupert, was Franz Boas's principal collaborator on the Northwest Coast. Hunt's insider status is evident in his 1902 photographs of a potlatch. His pictures are taken from a participant's point of view, not that of a studio photographer who arranges and poses his subjects. (104471)

10 / The slow film and large-format cameras carried on the expedition required considerable light to make a proper exposure. Most photographs were taken outdoors, but occasionally local architecture allowed for indoor photography with natural light. At certain seasons and times of day, shafts of sunlight could pass through smokeholes or doorways to illuminate interior scenes. (42923)

11 / Subjects had to hold perfectly still during the moment of exposure to avoid blurring the image, especially indoors. These two Koryak women were in the midst of weaving baskets when they posed for Jochelson's camera. Unfinished artifacts showing processes and techniques of manufacture are a hallmark of Boasian museum collections. (1576)

12 / Archaeological investigations were another component of the holistic method of collecting in early anthropology. In many areas, opportunities to excavate houses, shell heaps, and graves were infrequent. When such sites became available for digging, teams of workers were engaged to collect specimens of the past. (1591)

13 / Archaeologist Harlan I. Smith was the principal photographer on the Northwest Coast. He documented his work in great detail through sequences of photographs and accompanying notes and sketches. At the Great Fraser Midden in Eburne, British Columbia, Smith excavated the strata below cedar and maple stumps. (42964)

14 / In northeastern Siberia, acculturation was a complex web of influences. Over the centuries, members of some tribes had been Russified, while some Russians had adopted native customs. Jochelson encountered this Russian Orthodox priest, wearing native deerskin and drying fish, in a camp on the road near Gishiga. (22144)

15 / This charm—a post surrounded by sedge grass, horns, and antlers—was the old village guardian of the Koryak settlement of Kuel. A descendant of the village founder would smear the shrine with blood and fat to feed the guardian. In successful hunting years, a dog was sometimes offered as a sacrifice. Dogs were believed to guard the entrance to the country of the dead. (1573)

16 / Sakha blacksmiths held a social rank equivalent to that of shamans. They were considered gifted individuals with certain healing powers, and their workshops were sacred places. Blacksmiths of the ninth generation could forge rattling iron pendants for shamans' coats and drums without fear of harm from evil spirits. (1783)

17 / Jochelson collected this Sakha shaman's coat (AMNH 70/9070) and drum near Yakutsk. During healing rituals the shaman rode the drum like a horse, metal pendants rattling rhythmically. The two iron disks represent the sun and moon; the top disk was the ice hole through which the shaman dove into the spirit worlds. The chain was held by his assistant to ensure a safe return. Some Sakha shamans were female; most of those Jochelson met were male. (1832)

18 / "Of all the tribes of the extreme northeast of Siberia," Jochelson wrote, "the Yukaghir have fared the worst." Their population had declined steeply due to invasions, forced migrations, inter-marriage, assimilation, diseases, starvation, and extreme environmental conditions. The survivors inhabited the coldest and most severe terrain in the region. These Yukaghir women were photographed gathering berries. (11055)

19 / Bogoras photographed this Even woman with her reindeer at a fair in the maritime port of
Markovo. Some Siberian tribes, such as the Chukchi and Koryak, were divided into two groups:
Maritime divisions lived on the coast, fishing and hunting sea-mammals, while reindeer groups
followed the herds across the tundra. The populations mingled in towns, at markets, and
on festive occasions. (1310)

20 / A photograph represents a single moment frozen in time. Jochelson's photograph of a Koryak girl ice-fishing resembles a similar tableau in a Hall of Eskimos life group. Of the latter, J. D. Salinger wrote, "The best thing, though, in that museum was that everything always stayed right where it was. Nobody'd move. You could go there a hundred thousand times, and that Eskimo would still be just finished catching those two fish. . . . The only thing that would be different would be *you*." (4126)

21 / This 1895 photograph shows an Even family against a natural backdrop of snow. In many of Bogoras's photographs taken in the Arctic light of the far north, the horizon disappears in the diffuse glare of reflected light recorded by the camera. There is no vanishing point, and the isolated figures cast no shadows. (22410)

22 / Morris Jesup allowed Dina Jochelson-Brodskaya and Sofia Bogoras to join the expedition, without remuneration, on the condition that their scientific work become part of the expedition's results. Jochelson-Brodskaya photographed these two Yukaghir women as part of her study of the comparative anatomy of native women. (22160)

23 / Boas pioneered the statistical analysis of physiological measurements as changing over the course of an individual's life rather than as fixed data. In Worcester, Massachusetts, he had conducted anthropometrical research on young people in schools and gymnasia. Dina Jochelson-Brodskaya measured and photographed children and compared the growth of Yukaghir, Koryak, Itel'men (Kamchadal), and Chukchi individuals. (22154)

24 / Franz Boas was on the Northwest Coast during the winter ceremonial season of 1894. Many of the people he photographed at that time were wearing signs of their ritual status. A cedar bark neck ring was a mark of membership in one of the Kwakw<u>aka</u>'wakw "secret societies." (11549)

25 / Jack Tsacoola was photographed in Bella Bella by Harlan Smith during the summer of 1897. Tsacoola wore his trade-cloth kerchief tied in a distinctive circular knot. Its form was strikingly similar to the shape of cedar bark neck rings traditionally worn during rituals as a sign of initiation. (42840)

26 / In 1894 Boas wrote his wife, "The great drum of the Salvation Army exercises a strong influence here and has helped convert whole villages, especially because in their own beliefs the drum is supposed to attract supernatural help." In this 1897 photograph, Anna McKay wore her Salvation Army pin. (11724)

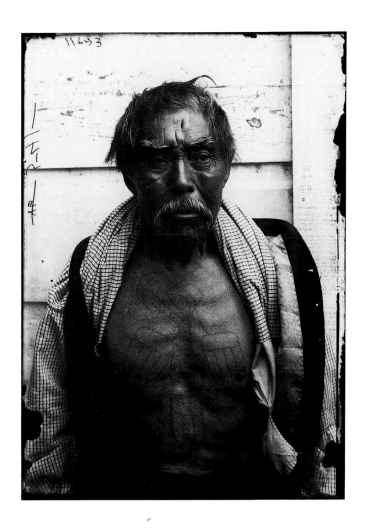

27 / Boas wrote home from the Skeena River on August 15, 1897, "I am rather satisfied with the results of my work here. . . . Although I should like to get more measurements, I think that the ethnological work is more important. . . . I made a very interesting series of face measurements, fifty-six altogether, which give me, as I expected, interesting clues to the meaning of local ornamentation." (11693)

28 / On the S.S. *Danube*, Harlan Smith and Franz Boas made a series of photographs and facial casts. Louisa of Massett, wearing a trade blanket, was paid $1.00 for a cast and the typical right and left profile photos. The figure of an unidentified man grinning in the background was poorly erased by an anonymous retoucher in an attempt to remove the image. (11736)

29 / Boas spent little time in the field during the expedition, and much of that waiting for steamers to arrive. On board the *Danube,* he wrote to his parents: "The only thing going on here is the gold fever. You cannot imagine how crazy the people are! Loads and loads of people go to Alaska. There will be a famine this winter. . . . The boats are terribly overcrowded." (11737)

30 / Boas considered that the form of an object alone is not truly indicative of its function and cultural relationships unless one knows its history and intended use. Bogoras labeled this image of masked figures on shipboard at Mariinsky Post "Protection against mosquitoes." (2643)

31 / The whale festival was the most important religious observance of the Maritime Koryak. A white whale captured by hunters was received as an honored guest. Its head was covered with a grass mask before it was butchered. After several days of ceremonials, its spirit was prepared to return to the sea. At this crucial moment, these two women wore grass masks for protection. If the ritual was successful, the whale would send its relatives to the village the next year. (1428)

32 / Unlike other peoples of the Northwest Coast, for whom spiritual privileges are inherited through birth or marriage, each individual among the Coast Salish must seek out and find his or her own guardian spirit. This board, photographed at Bay Centre, Washington, and then collected by Harlan Smith, may represent its owner's guardian spirit. The photograph was labeled "Tamanawas," evidently from a Chinook Jargon term for "being endowed with supernatural powers." (12126)

33 / The carved figure in this unidentified photograph may be a speaker's post or a figure representing a speaker or chief at a potlatch. Northwest Coast art scholar Bill Holm has identified the site as Fort Rupert. The bowls arranged on the ground suggest it was taken in 1898 at the time of a potlatch. (See also plate 48). (42991)

34 / Berthold Laufer, later sent by Boas on an expedition to China, studied the peoples of the Amur River region for the Jesup Expedition. These tribes have more in common with East Asian cultures than do Siberian peoples living farther north. Laufer hired studio photographer Emile Ninaud to take this portrait of a Nanai (Gold) family. (41614)

35 / Masks are rare in northeastern Siberia. In the Koryak village of Paren, Jochelson found wooden masks worn for amusement as well as for religious ceremonies. This photograph "represents three masked persons pretending to warm themselves by a woodpile. They received presents of pieces of sugar, tobacco, and ornaments, from the owner of the house. Thus they visited all the houses of the settlement." (1450)

36 / Before joining the Jesup Expedition, Waldemar Bogoras and Waldemar Jochelson had spent many years in Siberia as political exiles. As photographers they documented not only the native tribes they were sent to study but also exiled Russian intelligentsia and revolutionaries. (11091)

37 / In this Koryak raven game, the Mother-raven protected her young, lined up behind her, from the raven on the left, who threatened to eat them. Among the Chukchi and others, the raven was revered for bringing light to the people. The similar motifs of raven myths throughout the north Pacific supported the argument that there were longstanding relationships between the people of Siberia and the American Northwest. (4150)

38 / By practicing intensive hay-farming during the summer months, the Sakha are able to keep horses and cattle through the long Siberian winters. Jochelson reported that women generally preferred white horses. This wealthy bride posed in her finery, with her horse wearing richly decorated side and hind saddle covers. (1773)

39 / In their own language, the Yukaghir are called Odul, meaning "strong and powerful." They were once so numerous that other northern peoples called the stars "Yukaghir fire" after the many Yukaghir campfires visible at night. By 1900, only some two hundred souls remained; a century later there are more than a thousand. Jochelson's guides, seen here, lived in the settlements of the Kolyma River valley. They considered themselves, not the nomadic tundra Yukaghir, to be the true Odul. (22188)

40 / Dogs were used to pull sledges and for sacrifices, hunting, and skin clothing. Jochelson surveyed the Maritime Koryak of Penshina Bay and found that the average household owned ten dogs. He observed that ordinarily tame animals became excitable and ferocious when harnessed in a team, attacking men, reindeer, and other dogs. (1451)

41 / Jochelson wrote to Franz Boas in April 1902, "This is the most difficult journey I have ever made. . . . Travel conditions to the northern districts of Yakutsk province were very bad this year. The eastern Yukaghir suffered from hunger and life there was very sad. The deep snow made our travel from Verkhne to Sredne Kolymsk difficult. Fishing had been so unsuccessful in and around Sredne Kolymsk that people were forced to kill their sled dogs." (2A13549)

42 / Because of carnivores and permafrost, above-ground graves were widespread. Jochelson photographed this Evenk shaman's coffin, made of sewn willow boards, on the Kolyma tundra around 1897. Its platform had collapsed. The carved birds were probably divers, often associated with Evenk shamans during their spiritual flights to other worlds. (11023)

43 / Young Kwakwa̱ka'wakw men were seized by the powerful cannibal spirit Baxwbakwalanux-wsiwe' and were taken to the woods in order to become *hamatsa* (initiates of the cannibal spirits). An initiate's theatrical cries of *"Hap, hap, hap!"* (meaning "Eat!") indicated his supposed desire for human flesh. (22853)

44 / The *hamatsa* performance marked the initiate's gradual return to society. Wearing only hemlock branches, he acted wild and had to be restrained. During the ceremonies, these branches were replaced by red cedar bark. After three dancers in bird masks had performed, the *hamatsa* was tamed by the sound of shaking rattles and the gestures of a female attendant. (22891)

45 / Indian Point (Unisak) was located near the farthest eastern point of Asia. Directly across the
Bering Strait from St. Lawrence Island, the settlement was a regional center for maritime trade.
Bogoras made a large number of phonograph recordings and photographs there among the
Asian Eskimos. This wrestling match and other games took place at a festival gathering. (2506)

46 / Harlan Smith captured a moment of the traditional gambling often held during potlatches. The inability of the camera to record fast motion is evident in the blurred image of the drum being beaten. Note the two boys in straw hat and scarf on the far right of the frame. (42999)

47 / The same two boys on the right of the previous image can be clearly seen on the left of this unidentified photograph. The two pictures, taken moments apart, form a continuous panoramic scene when placed side by side. The second shot was probably taken by O. C. Hastings. (128022)

48 / At the 1898 Fort Rupert potlatch photographed by Harlan Smith, women's goods were laid out before being exchanged. The bowls and other items were arrayed in an ostentatious display accentuating the wealth of the host. In potlatch settings, unlike the contrived scenes that photographers had to arrange for life groups, objects were already arranged in visual displays. (42992)

49 / The Sakha honored the coming of spring in annual festivals called *ysakh*. These important religious occasions provided opportunities for courtship and socializing. "The whole day," Jochelson wrote, "passed with songs, round dances, games, races and other contests, and shamanistic performances." Uniformed observers can be seen in the background watching the proceedings. (1803)

50 / Participants in spring *ysakh* festivals drank offerings of *kumiss,* a sacred brew of fermented mare's milk, from special vessels called *choron.* Jochelson believed the ritual was dying out, but in modern times *ysakh* has played a key role in Sakha cultural revival. The ceremony pictured here was held early to accommodate Jochelson's travel schedule. (1796)

51 / The Hall of Northwest Coast Indians at the American Museum of Natural History, constructed of artifacts, models, and murals representing traditional cultures, has evoked deeply personal responses from visitors over the decades. The anthropologist Claude Lévi-Strauss spoke for many of them when he described his magical, almost religious fascination with its art and ambience. (33003)

52 / As Christianity spread, concerns with burial resulted in mortuary adaptations for some of the converted on both sides of the north Pacific. In this Sakha cemetery, the slanted crosspiece of the Russian Orthodox church is visible along with several *sergey* (posts carved to represent traditional Sakha drinking vessels.) (See plate 50.) (1778)

53 / On the Northwest Coast, older funerary practices such as burying bodies in canoes or trees were gradually being supplanted by burials in graveyards. In Fort Rupert, in front of a white picket fence, large carved coppers—traditional signs of Indian wealth and status—were erected over graves to indicate the rank of the deceased. (43004)

54 / In the field, anthropologists photographed objects in the collection being demonstrated in order to document their manner of use and for reference in making museum models. The Evenk shaman who posed for this picture with drum and full costume may have been Athanasy, nicknamed Mash'ka, whom Jochelson employed as a guide. (1610)

55 / Jochelson wrote that Athanasy shamanized with "wild onomatopoeic screams, whistling, grinding of teeth and terrible facial contortions." This fearless and furious performance unnerved and exhausted his spectators, including Jochelson, who noted that afterwards "Athanasy became quite calm and told me that he had seen my path and that I should happily return home." (1611)

56 / At the same time that new architectural forms, like the steeple in the background of this photo-graph from Bella Bella, emerged on the Northwest Coast, some older buildings were dismantled and shipped to museums. Harlan Smith collected all four corner posts of this house. Two remain on display in the American Museum of Natural History. (42853)

57 / The anthropologists on the Jesup Expedition commissioned and collected scale models of objects that would have been too large to transport to New York. Here a group of Asian Eskimo men at Indian Point on the Bering Strait are at work making a miniature wooden model of a traditional building for the American Museum's collection. (1356)

58 / Harlan Smith wrote to Boas on April 27, 1898: "At Kamloops got . . . deer skin, scraper, stone in handle—birch bark basket and stone scraper. For these last 4 I paid $4.00. This seemed high but I photoed the woman scraping skin and thought you might need a skin and scraper for the group showing squaw scraping skin." (333415)

59 / The woman photographed at Kamloops by Smith was wearing an imported dress, while the mannequin based on the photograph is in deerskin. By this time, virtually all Nlaka'pamux wore western-style clothing. They actively participated in the representation of their tribal past by selling traditional items to the American Museum and posing for photographs. (42930)

60 / Bogoras and Jochelson exposed a series of photographs of men wearing traditional armor and fighting mock battles for the camera. The playful attitude of these laughing warriors reveals photographic representation for the museum as an act of theater, a collaboration between anthropologist and native host to construct images of the past. (2723)

Afterword: The Present and Future of the Jesup Expedition Photographs

Laurel Kendall

I F   T H I S exploration of the Jesup Expedition photographs has illuminated the intentions of the early twentieth-century anthropologists who made them, if these photographs now reflect the shadow images of those who composed their frames and clicked the shutters, then Barbara Mathé and Thomas Ross Miller have succeeded at their task. But if the old ethnographic photograph is an imperfect witness, a suspect witness, does that make it always an invalid witness? Much depends upon the questions the viewer asks of the photograph.

On the Northwest Coast, expedition anthropologists looked backward, through the photograph, to a "traditional way of life" they could restore in museum dioramas, where the manikins would be dressed in bark cloth and skins, rather than in store-bought cotton and wool. Today, these same photographs gain in historic value precisely because their subjects come to us in turn-of-the-century skirts and trousers. We see people inhabiting their own moment, forced into new ways of living but proudly maintaining traditions despite government and missionary opposition.

Along the Northwest Coast at the time of the Jesup Expedition, "tradition" seems to have become a self-conscious category not only for anthropologists, but for the native peoples who were their subjects. Might the participants in a potlatch, solemn before the ethnographer's camera, be imagining another time, a past that legitimized the ceremonies, songs, and stories that confer identity in an uncertain present?

The Siberian photographs, taken as a whole, provide far less visual evidence of contact, even allowing, as Miller and Mathé suggest, photographers—on both sides of the Bering Strait—to excise modern things from their frames. But history is an omnipresent process. The very possibility of scientific expeditions to study Siberian people followed upon the Russian Empire's having closed in upon them with Cossacks, missionaries, and epidemic diseases. Miller and Mathé end their essay with the teasing suggestion that the recently pacified Chukchi warriors who posed so enthusiastically for the camera were asserting their own history, witnessing with their armor, weapons, and body postures a time that had only recently become "the past."

At what moment do a people begin to define themselves with reference to a lost time? Perhaps this moment had not yet arrived for the people we see in many of the Siberian photographs, posed in reindeer camps and fishing villages. It is their descendants who seek the lost time when they gaze at these same images from across a brutal century.

In the spring of 1996, Gavril Nikolaevich Kurilov, one of a small number of surviving Yukaghir people and their leading intellectual, visited the American Museum of Natural History on a very special mission. He and his colleague, Vladimir Karlampovich Ivanov, had translated Jochelson's classic monograph on the Yukaghir (1926) into the Russian and Yukaghir languages. They saw Jochelson's work as a testimony to the richness of Yukaghir culture before Soviet times; an accessible translation would help the Yukaghir recapture pride in their own history and culture after decades of forced assimilation. Some of the book's intended readers would be Yukaghir schoolchildren.

Mr. Kurilov and Mr. Ivanov came to New York to examine, first hand, the objects illustrated in the book in line drawings and to select photographs from the Museum Library's archive for the publication. But Mr. Kurilov also looked upon the photo archive as a kind of family album. He wondered if he would be able to recognize his own kin.

In our time, the photographs in the Museum archive, together with the objects in our collections, take on the quality of a time capsule. They slept Sleeping Beauty's sleep for nearly a century. Now, they have become resources for a global community of scholars, the like of which could not have been imagined at the time of the Jesup Expedition. Young anthropologists, preparing for fieldwork in Siberia, visit our collections. Sometimes they go to the field with photographs of objects and archival images which they use as prompts in their own fieldwork and bestow upon local museums. Scholars from the Russian Federation have renewed ties with the American Museum of Natural History that began with the Jesup Expedition one hundred years ago. Some of our visitors, like Mr. Kurilov, a Yukaghir, and Mr. Ivanov, a Sakha, are native scholars concerned with cultural revival. Photographs of objects in our collections have inspired the work of contemporary artisans in the Sakha Republic. A spokeswoman for the Itel'men people recently told a Museum curator that archival photographs provided by Columbia University professor David Koester and his team were being "breathed back to life" in her community. As witnesses to a lost time, however imperfect, the photographs in the Jesup Archive are part of the unfolding history of our own time.

I wish to thank Marjorie Mandelstam Balzer for her thoughtful comments on this essay.

Acknowledgments

THE EXHIBITION *"Drawing Shadows to Stone": Photographing North Pacific Peoples, 1897–1902* and this publication are the result of the collaborative efforts of many people. We are grateful to the Board of Trustees of the American Museum of Natural History, President Ellen Futter, and Dean of Science Craig Morris for their support of this project. The authors began this research as part of the Jesup II initiative originating at the Arctic Studies Center, National Museum of Natural History, Smithsonian Institution. The present study of the photographic collection grew out of a paper presented in 1993 to the American Anthropological Association, on a panel devoted to the archival resources of the Jesup North Pacific Expedition.

As guest curators, we thank Laurel Kendall for organizing and managing the Jesup centenary project at the American Museum of Natural History, and for the opportunity to participate and contribute. This exhibition and publication would not have come about without her expertise, vision, and perseverance. We also thank Stanley Freed for sharing with us his expert knowledge and advice. Paula Wilhelme performed the invaluable service of carefully compiling a database of the photographs and their annotations, correcting inaccuracies in the record along the way. We thank our many colleagues at the American Museum of Natural History, especially Denis Finnin, Jackie Beckett, and Craig Chesek in the Photography Studio for their heroic printing. We are indebted to many people in the Department of Library Services, Special Collections, and the Department of Anthropology. We thank them all for their collegial endeavors; special mention must go to Carmen Collazo, Joel Sweimler, Andrea LaSala, Sarah Granato Yeates, Tom Baione, Lisa Stock, Paul Beelitz, Belinda Kaye, Anibal Rodriguez, Laila Williamson, and Ann Wright-Parsons. Judith Ostrowitz of the Brooklyn Museum, Nelson Hancock of Columbia University, and Evalyn Stone of the Metropolitan Museum of Art offered helpful comments on the manuscript. Special thanks also go to David Koester, C. Y. Wilder, Kris Waldherr, and John Swenson.

We would like to name here a few of the key players at the American Museum of Natural History, whose efforts greatly contributed to the making of the exhibition. Larry Langham, the exhibition designer, turned the ideas into reality. A few of the others whose inspiration and indefatigible work made the project successful include Kevin Walker, Bill Weinstein, Larry Van Praag, Chris Toy, Judith Levinson and her staff of outstanding conservators, Barbara Rhodes, Willard Whitson, Elaine Charnov, Teddy Yoshikami, Rose Wadsworth, and Ann Fitzgerald.

Much time passes between a catalogue going to press and the opening of an exhibition. We thank all of those who are not named here. Any errors in judgment or fact are, of course, entirely our own.

Barbara Mathé and Thomas Ross Miller
Guest Curators

In 1898, in the Siberian region of Verkhoyansk, Dina Jochelson-Brodskaya and Waldemar Jochelson posed in arctic costume against a painted background.

References

Archival sources are identified in the text as follows:

DA for the American Museum of Natural History Department of Anthropology Archives;

AMNH for the American Museum of Natural History Archives.

ALLOULA, MALEK

1986   *The Colonial Harem.* Translated by Myrna
        Godzich and Wlad Godzich. Minneapolis:
        University of Minnesota Press.

BALZER, MARJORIE

1992   "Introduction to Cultural History of the Yakut
        (Sakha) People," *Anthropology and Archeology
        of Eurasia* 31(2):4–9.

BARKHATOVA, ELENA

1992   "Realism and Document: Photography as Fact."
        In *Photography in Russia,* ed. David Elliott.
        Berlin: Thames and Hudson.

BENJAMIN, WALTER

1977   "Walter Benjamin's Short History of
        Photography," *Artforum* 15:46–51. Translated
        by Phil Patton. (Originally published in 1931.)

BLACK, LYDIA

1988   "Peoples of the Amur and Maritime Regions."
        In *Crossroads of Continents,* ed. William Fitzhugh
        and Aron Crowell. Washington, D.C.:
        Smithsonian Institution Press.

BLACKMAN, MARGARET B.

1980   "Posing the American Indians," *Natural History*
        89:68–75.

1981   *Window on the Past: The Photographic Ethno-
        history of the Northern and Kaigani Haida.*
        National Museum of Man Mercury Series,
        Canadian Ethnology Service Paper No. 74.
        Ottawa: National Museums of Canada.

BOAS, FRANZ

1887   "The Occurrence of Similar Inventions in Areas
        Widely Apart," *Science* 9:485–86.

1903   "The Jesup North Pacific Expedition," *The
        American Museum Journal* 3(5):72–119.

1940   *Race, Language and Culture.* New York:
        Macmillan Company. Franz Boas, series ed.

1898–   *Memoirs of the American Museum of Natural
1930   History,* Jesup North Pacific Expedition, vols.
        1–11. New York: American Museum of Natural
        History.

CODERE, HELEN, ED.

1966   *Kwakiutl Ethnography: Franz Boas.* Chicago:
        University of Chicago Press.

COLE, DOUGLAS

1982   "Franz Boas and the Bella Coola in Berlin,"
        Northwest Anthropological Research Notes
        16(2):115–24.

1985   *Captured Heritage: The Scramble for Northwest
        Coast Artifacts.* Vancouver, B.C.: Douglas and
        McIntyre; Seattle: University of Washington
        Press.

COLE, DOUGLAS, AND IRA CHAIKIN

1990   *An Iron Hand Upon the People: The Law Against
        the Potlatch on the Northwest Coast.* Vancouver,
        B.C.: Douglas and McIntyre; Seattle: University
        of Washington Press.

DEXTER, RALPH W.

1976   "The Role of F. W. Putnam in Developing

Anthropology at the American Museum of Natural History," *Curator* 19:303–10.

EDWARDS, ELIZABETH

1992   "Introduction." In *Anthropology and Photography, 1860–1920,* ed. Elizabeth Edwards, pp. 3–17. New Haven: Yale University Press.

ELLIOTT, DAVID, ED.

1992   *Photography in Russia, 1840–1940.* Berlin: Thames and Hudson.

EMMONS, GEORGE THORNTON

1991   *The Tlingit Indians.* Edited by Frederica de Laguna. New York: American Museum of Natural History; Seattle: University of Washington Press.

FITZHUGH, WILLIAM, AND ARON CROWELL, EDS.

1988   *Crossroads of Continents: Cultures of Siberia and Alaska.* Washington, D.C.: Smithsonian Institution Press.

FITZHUGH, WILLIAM, AND SUSAN A. KAPLAN

1982   *Inua: Spirit World of the Bering Sea Eskimo.* Washington, D.C.: Smithsonian Institution Press.

FREED, STANLEY A., RUTH S. FREED, AND LAILA WILLIAMSON

1988a   "Capitalist Philanthropy and Russian Revolutionaries: The Jesup North Pacific Expedition (1897–1902)," *American Anthropologist* 90(1): 7–24.

1988b   "Scholars Amid Squalor," *Natural History* 97(3):60–68.

GURVICH, I. S., AND L. P. KUZMINA

1985   'W. G. Bogoras et W. I. Jochelson: Deux eminents représentants de l'ethnographie Russe," *Inter-Nord* 17:145–51.

HILL-TOUT, CHARLES

1978   *The Salish People.* Vol. I: *Thompson.* Edited by Ralph Maud. Vancouver, B.C.: Talonbooks. (Originally published in 1899.)

IOKHEL'SON'-BRODSKAYA, DINA L.

1907   "K'antropologii zhenshin' plemen krainyago severo-vostoka Sibiri [Towards an anthropology of native women]," *Russkii antropologicheskii zhurnal* 25(1):1–87.

JACKNIS, IRA

1984   "Franz Boas and Photography," *Studies in Visual Communication* 10(1):2–60.

1985   "Franz Boas and Exhibits: On the Limitations of the Museum Method of Anthropology." In *Objects and Others: Essays on Museums and Material Culture,* ed. George W. Stocking, Jr., pp. 75–111. Madison: University of Wisconsin Press.

JOCHELSON, WALDEMAR

1926   *The Yukaghir and Yukaghirized Tungus.* Anthropological Papers of the American Museum of Natural History, vol. 9. New York: American Museum of Natural History.

1928   *Peoples of Asiatic Russia.* New York: American Museum of Natural History.

1933   *The Yakut.* Anthropological Papers of the American Museum of Natural History, vol. 33(2). New York: American Museum of Natural History.

JONAITIS, ALDONA

1988   *From the Land of the Totem Poles: The Northwest Coast Indian Art Collection at the American Museum of Natural History.* New York: American Museum of Natural History; Seattle: University of Washington Press.

JONAITIS, ALDONA, ED.

1991   *Chiefly Feasts: The Enduring Kwakiutl Potlatch.* New York: American Museum of Natural History; Seattle:University of Washington Press.

KENDALL, LAUREL

1988   "Young Laufer on the Amur." In *Crossroads of Continents: Cultures of Siberia and Alaska,* ed. William Fitzhugh and Aron Crowell. Washington, D.C.: Smithsonian Institution Press.

KRACAUER, SIEGFRIED

1995   "Photography." In *The Mass Ornament: Weimar Essays,* pp. 47–63. Translated and edited by Thomas Y. Levin. Cambridge, MA: Harvard University Press. (Originally published in 1963.)

KRUPNIK, IGOR

1993   *Arctic Adaptations: Native Whalers and Reindeer Herders of Northern Eurasia.* Hanover, NH: University Press of England.

KUNDERA, MILAN

1981   *The Book of Laughter and Forgetting.* New York: Penguin Books.

LYMAN, CHRISTOPHER M.

1982   *The Vanishing Race and Other Illusions: Photographs of Indians by Edward S. Curtis.* New York: Pantheon Books.

MASON, O. T.

1887   "The Occurrence of Similar Inventions in Areas Widely Apart," *Science* 9:534–35.

MATHÉ, BARBARA

1996   "Jessie Tarbox Beals' Photographs for the 1904 Louisiana Purchase Exposition," *Visual Resources Association Bulletin* 23(4).

MATHÉ, BARBARA, AND THOMAS ROSS MILLER

1997   "Symbols of the Past: Images in Museum Representation." In *The Legacy of the Jesup North Pacific Expedition,* ed. Igor Krupnik and William Fitzhugh. Washington, D.C.: Smithsonian Institution Press.

MILLER, THOMAS ROSS

1992   "The Evidence of Instruments," *Anthropology and Humanism Quarterly* 17(2):49–60.

MORRIS, ROSALIND C.

1994   *New Worlds from Fragments: Film, Ethnography, and the Representation of Northwest Coast Cultures.* Boulder, CO: Westview Press.

POWELL, J. W.

1887   "Museums of Ethnology and Their Classification," *Science* 9:612–14.

ROHNER, RONALD, ED.

1969   *The Ethnography of Franz Boas.* Chicago: University of Chicago Press.

SALINGER, J. D.

1991   *The Catcher in the Rye.* Boston: Little, Brown. (Originally published in 1951.)

SLEZKINE, YURI

1994   *Arctic Mirrors: Russia and the Small Peoples of the North.* Ithaca, NY: Cornell University Press.

STOCKING, GEORGE, JR.

1968   *Race, Culture, and Evolution: Essays in the History of Anthropology.* Chicago: University of Chicago Press.

STOCKING, GEORGE W., JR., ED.

1974   *The Shaping of American Anthropology, 1883–1911: A Franz Boas Reader.* New York: Basic Books.

TAUSSIG, MICHAEL T.

1993   *Mimesis and Alterity: A Particular History of the Senses.* New York: Routledge.

TCHEN, JOHN KUO WEI

1984   *Genthe's Photographs of San Francisco's Old Chinatown.* New York: Dover Publications.

TROUBETZKOY, WLADIMIR

1980   "Les Décembristes, ethnographes de la Sibérie," *L'Ethnographie* 1980–81:135–73.

VAKHTIN, NIKOLAI

1994   "Franz Boas and the Shaping of the Jesup North Pacific Expedition, 1895–1900: A Russian Perspective." Manuscript (44 pages).

Index

Boldface numbers refer to pages with text illustrations.